MW01092988

TALES FROM THE
BOSTON COLLEGE HOCKEY
LOCKER ROOM

TALES FROM THE
BOSTON COLLEGE HOCKEY
LOCKER ROOM

A COLLECTION OF THE GREATEST EAGLES HOCKEY STORIES EVER TOLD

BY TOM BURKE AND
REID OSLIN

SPORTS
PUBLISHING

Sports Publishing books may be purchased in bulk at special discounts for sales promotion, corporate gifts, fund-raising, or educational purposes. Special editions can also be created to specifications. For details, contact the Special Sales Department, Sports Publishing, 307 West 36th Street, 11th Floor, New York, NY 10018 or sportspubbooks@skyhorsepublishing.com.

Sports Publishing® is a registered trademark of Skyhorse Publishing, Inc.®, a Delaware corporation.

Visit our website at www.sportspubbooks.com.

10 9 8 7 6 5 4 3 2 1

Library of Congress Cataloging-in-Publication Data is available on file.
Cover series design by Tom Lau
Cover photo credit AP Images

Print ISBN: 978-1-61321-649-1
Ebook ISBN: 978-1-61321-676-7

Printed in the United States of America

CONTENTS

A Note from the Authors

College hockey is a unique sport. It is "big time," with many of its best players going on to win Olympic medals and to carve out successful professional careers. Yet it is a "small" sport as well. Relatively few schools have chosen to make the game a part of their athletic tradition and to invest the time and treasure required for success. So the college hockey community is a tightly knit one. We're an extended family. We're all in this together.

The people of Boston College comprise an important branch of college hockey's extended family. BC coach Jerry York told us that observing the players on his teams was like watching a band of brothers who share the same lineage. While each one has his own unique personality, you can tell that he belongs, that he's had the same upbringing, adheres to the same values, and displays the same mannerisms as those on his team and those who've come before him.

We agree, and it's not only the players of Jerry's generation. Everyone who has played Boston's sport at Boston's college shares that special bond. It doesn't matter if he laced up his skates to do hockey battle in the Boston Arena, in McHugh Forum, or in Kelley Rink. This book tells the stories of many of those BC hockey men. We hope you enjoy meeting them.

Tom Burke
Reid Oslin
May 2014

Acknowledgments

This book would not have been possible without the enthusiastic support and contributions of time, memories, and personal memorabilia that we received from many players, coaches, administrators, family members of deceased players, and hockey people. Many, but not all, of their names are mentioned in the book. While they are too numerous to list here, we would like to extend a special thanks to the following for their assistance: Bobby Allen, Dan Bertram, Mike Brennan, Greg Brown, Steve Bushee, Eddie Carroll, Mike Cavanaugh, Steve Cedorchuk, Christina Coleman, Jack Cronin, Tommy Cross, Ted Crowley, Tony Dello Russo, David Emma, Brian Gionta, Jim Greene, Matt Greene, Bob Griffin, John Hegarty, Bill Hogan Jr., Bill Hogan III, Jack Kelley, Krys Kolanos, Warren Lewis, Jim Logue, Barry MacCarthy, Tom Martin, Marty McInnis, Tom Mellor, Jim Mullen, Joe Mullen, Tom Murray, Rev. Frank Parker, S.J., Rev. Anthony Penna, Tom Peters, Andy Powers, Mike Powers, Matt Price, Marty Reasoner, Mark Riley, Carmine Sarno, Richard Schoenfeld, Vin Shanley, Dan Shea, Tim Sheehy, Charlie Sullivan, Giles Threadgold, and Coach Jerry York.

A special word of thanks goes out to all the folks in the BC Sports Media Relations Department, especially Chris Cameron, Tim Clark, and Mark Majewski, who supported this project from the beginning.

As always, the University Archives staff—most notably, Assistant Archivist Shelley Barber—of Boston College's John J. Burns Library was most helpful in collecting photographs and material from the Eagles' glorious hockey history. Likewise, we cannot write a publication of this scope without a tip of the cap to the late, great historian of Boston College athletics, Dr. Nathaniel Hasenfus, '22, whose marvelous 1943 book, *Athletics at Boston College*, once again provided substantial information and insight into the early days of athletics at the Heights.

Another invaluable source of material on the beginnings of hockey in Boston was "Long Before Orr," the superbly researched essay by University of New Hampshire professor Steve Hardy in *The Rock, The Curse, and The Hub: A Random History of Boston Sports.*

We are especially grateful to Dick Kelley and Candace Kelley McLaughlin, who shared their extensive scrapbooks and scores of mementoes chronicling their father's great career at Boston College; also, Coach Len Ceglarski; Joe Burke, the son of former Coach Bernie Burke; Larry Sanford, son of Lawrence "Pete" Sanford; and BC Hall of Famer Sherm Saltmarsh—all of whom generously provided scrapbooks and other memorabilia of Boston College Hockey; and Tom Leehan, whose collection of Boston College game programs, yearbooks, and other sports publications is second to none.

1

2001, AN ICE ODYSSEY
End of a Long Road, Beginning of Another

Exhausted and emotionally drained, the Boston College hockey players trudged off the ice of the Pepsi Center in Albany, New York. Their two-goal, third-period lead over the defending national champion North Dakota had vanished in a span of three minutes and six seconds. The gung ho Sioux had overwhelmed them in the offensive zone, crashing the net and hurling puck after puck on goaltender Scott Clemmensen.

North Dakota's winning score seemed imminent and inevitable. But the final buzzer got there first. The score remained 2-2. The national championship would be a 3-2 decision, decided in sudden-death overtime. Just like four years before, in Boston.

Evil spirits bearing bitter memories—of defeat in each of the past three NCAA Frozen Four Tournaments—followed the players to the locker room and mounted their own assaults. Would victory be snatched away from them yet again?

Not this time.

"We're not going to lose this game," said senior Marty Hughes. "We've come too far. We're not going to lose. All we've got to do is score one goal. We're not feeling sorry for ourselves."

Hughes was one of eight fourth-year players on the squad and perhaps the quietest of them all.

But not this time.

Hughes had been a highly recruited defenseman when he came to Boston College four years before. Midway through his junior year, the coaches moved him up to the forward lines, where they needed depth and checking help. Like many of those who'd follow him in future years, with Hughes it was everything for the team.

And that year, it was everyone on the team for Marty Hughes. About three months previously, when his mother Eileen had passed away, the team's seniors went down to Long Island to stay with Marty and his family. They'd been there for him, and now he was here for them.

"We're not going to lose this game."

And they didn't. Scott Clemmensen, the senior goalie from Iowa who had been in net for all three Final Four defeats, gloved the first shot, two minutes into the overtime, by the Sioux's Bryan Lundbohm. Two minutes later he repulsed a shot through traffic off the stick of David Lundbohm.

The Eagles dashed up ice. To Tony Voce, to Chuck Kobasew, and then to Krys Kolanos went the puck. Over the blue line and down the left boards flew the long-striding sophomore from Calgary. He turned one defender, cut to the center, switched to his forehand, and slipped the puck beneath the gloved left hand of goaltender Karl Goehring. Victory. At last.

Fifty-two years after Boston College had become the first Eastern team to win the NCAA hockey championship, the Eagles became the first Eastern team of the new millennium to climb to that pinnacle of their sport.

Nineteen times in those fifty-two years, they had entered the tournament and did not win it. In 2001, the Eagles defeated all of the teams that had eliminated them in the preceding three NCAA Tournaments: Maine, Michigan, and North Dakota.

"We were there to take care of unfinished business," said defenseman Bobby Allen. He, like Clemmensen, had lived through those three previous disappointments.

The game-winning goal was the final one Kolanos would score as an Eagle, as he elected to turn professional after that season.

"It was special to be a part of winning that first championship in fifty-two years," he said. "And you feel a part of all the ones they've won since. The guys believe. There's a higher expectation now."

April 7, 2001, marked the end of a quest that had taken more than half a century. It also marked the start of another journey that brought Boston College to the top of the college hockey world three more times in the next eleven years.

BC's Brian Gionta skates around the ice with the 2001 NCAA National Championship trophy. (*Photo courtesy of Boston College Sports Media Relations*)

2

THE EARLY DAYS OF BOSTON COLLEGE HOCKEY

ICE POLO: THE FORERUNNER GAME

One of the first team sports organized at BC's original James Street campus in Boston's South End was ice polo. It was an on-ice version of roller polo, which had taken hold in the Boston area at some time in the 1880s. The game used a rubber ball and had five players on a side, each of whom wielded a mallet-like stick.

The president of BC at the time, Rev. Timothy Brosnahan, S.J., authorized the formation of a team in the hopes that it would give the growing Catholic school better visibility within the community. He even authorized the use of the school's colors for a publicity campaign.

The first captain of ice polo at BC was William Lyons, who later turned down contract offers from three major league baseball teams to enter the seminary and study for the priesthood. The first team manager was James O'Connell, who doubled as the college's publicist.

There were eight candidates for that first team in 1896, and Fr. Brosnahan sent them off to Wright & Ditson's Sporting Goods store in downtown Boston to purchase skates, shin guards, and sticks. Reportedly, the school's business manager was aghast when he saw the bill—an early lesson in the high costs of college athletics.

Fr. Brosnahan was the first chief administrator to champion athletics at Boston College. He also built a small gymnasium in the school's only building and purchased an athletic field in the city's South End for the use of fall and spring season teams.

Since there was no indoor ice rink in the city at that time, the team played its games on Wednesday and Saturday afternoons—weather permitting—at either Franklin Park or a flooded lot located behind Boston City Hospital.

ICE HOCKEY: THE MONTREAL GAME

Ice polo was soon swept aside in Boston by "The Montreal Game," which had originated at McGill University. It used a puck rather than a ball. There were seven men on a side in those days—four forwards, two defensemen, and a goalie. Boston College took up the new game in the winter of 1897–98. Games were played on ponds or flooded fields. Venues included Lake Quannapowitt and Crystal Lake in Wakefield; Horn Pond in Woburn; Turner's Pond in Milton; and the popular Franklin Field.

Hockey in Boston took a big forward leap when the first Boston Arena was built on Saint Botolph Street in 1910. Saint Michael's College of Montreal played in the first game against the Boston Hockey Club before a crowd of four thousand, and the sport was underway in the Hub.

College hockey's first superstar was Hobey Baker, a Concord, Massachusetts, lad who played for Princeton up until 1914 and then for the prestigious Saint Nicholas Club of New York. Ralph Winsor, coach of Harvard from 1902 to 1917, frequently faced the "clever dodger" Baker and devised the first alignment of two defensemen stationed side-by-side. This "Winsor system" was an effective countermeasure to Baker's skating and stickhandling wizardry.

In 1917–1918, Boston College formalized its varsity hockey team and began intercollegiate competition. The team had an outdoor practice rink just northeast of the Tower Building, occupying the piece of land that is now the Rose Garden of St. Mary's Hall. It was watered and scraped by hand to maintain the ice surface. The team also held occasional practices in the Boston Arena.

The first game result entered in the Boston College hockey history books shows a 7-1 victory over Harvard Radio School on January 9, 1918.

Boston College's first campus rink was a temporary outdoor facility on the current site of the St. Mary's Hall Rose Garden. (*Photo courtesy of Boston College University Archives*)

In that game, a player named Eddie Enright had three goals—the first hat trick in Boston College history. Enright soon transferred to Harvard and finished out his playing career as a member of the Crimson.

Harvard Radio School was one of two such institutions run by the US Navy for the training of Morse code operators. War with Germany was imminent, and America joined the carnage in Europe less than two months after that first hockey game. Only four more ice hockey contests involving Boston College would take place over the next two years. The Great War curtailed sporting programs at most colleges, but after the armistice, colleges like Harvard, Tufts, and BC all announced plans to return to prewar schedules.

The first Boston Arena burned to the ground in December 1918, and for a season indoor hockey survived at the Pavilion, a small facility near MIT. The new Boston Arena opened on Saint Botolph Street in 1920 under general manager George V. Brown, who was also director of athletics at the Boston Athletic Association. The Arena was the home of the Boston Bruins until the larger Boston Garden was built in 1928.

In 1919–20, hockey on the Heights resumed with a seven-game schedule. The first was at the Pavilion. It was a 4-2 BC triumph over the Yankee Division, the Massachusetts 26th Infantry comprising boys from National Guard units around the Bay State.

CAPTAINS AND STARS OF THE ROARING TWENTIES

The first captain of hockey at Boston College was Walter "Dido" Falvey, a five-foot-tall, but wiry athlete from Brighton. In spite of his size, Falvey was a tough competitor. "He looks like a grouch, but appearances are deceitful," the Sub Turri yearbook said of the first hockey captain, who was also on the premed track. He was cited as an "exceptional captain, coach and speedster of our seven." The team recruited the star kicker of the football team, Jimmy Fitzpatrick, to tend goal.

In 1920, another, larger, outdoor rink was constructed on Alumni Field (the current site of Stokes Hall), and the team expanded its schedule, playing teams from Dartmouth, Bates, and Amherst, but still scheduling games with local amateur squads, including the Shoe Trades Union, who easily brought the Eagles to heel in defeating them 7-1. Throughout the 1920s, the Eagles' schedules also included games against the Boston Athletic Association, St. Nick's, and Canadian schools like McGill, Toronto, Queen's, and Montreal University.

Catholic families stocked the Eagle teams of those years, and many faithful churchgoers became faithful fans. The biggest draws included the five Morrissey brothers, Leo Hughes, and James "Sonny" Foley. The Morrissey family of Medford takes the unofficial title of "First Family of Boston College Hockey," as five brothers played varsity hockey at the school in the early years of the sport. James (1918–19), Frank (1917–21, captain in 1919–20); Leonard (1919–23); William (1922–26); and Arthur (1925–29, captain in 1928–29) all wore the BC sweaters.

Hughes, the team captain in both 1921 and 1922, also played for the BAA Unicorns after his Boston College days. The Unicorns were a power in the "Eastern Loop" of the US Amateur Hockey Association circuit. Their most hated rivals were the Pittsburgh Yellow Jackets, that era's version of the 1960s Cornell teams built by Ned Harkness. The Yellow Jackets stocked up with Canadian stars like Lionel Conacher and Baldy Cotton, and won the league title in 1924 and 1925.

The Boston press railed against Pittsburgh. The *Boston Herald*'s "Bob Dunbar" columnist wondered why Boston hockey was involved with the Yellow Jackets at all, pointing that Pittsburgh was a team of "traveling mercenaries, who practically all are of Canadian background and training." Sportswriter W.W. Mullins wrote "with their tactics of slashing their opponents around their thighs and ankle, hooks around the face . . . and worst of all, the expert manner in which most of them could stick [spear] and use the butt ends of their mashies in massaging the ribs of their rivals."

Hughes was fresh out of Boston College and a darling of Boston hockey fans when he played for the Unicorns. He became the biggest victim of Pittsburgh's mayhem in 1925 when Joe Sills butt-ended him in the face. The assault required the removal of Hughes's right eye and the possible loss of his left. The league president, a Pittsburgh guy, responded to protests by stating, "Hockey is not a parlor game."

Educators at the secondary-school level took notice too. The director of Boston's public schools subsequently warned his underlings to cut back on the violence or he would ban hockey, just as he'd recently done to another sport: basketball.

By 1927, the Eagles had chosen Foley, their former captain, star, and Class of '25 member, to coach the team. "An ideal coach," wrote the *Sub Turri* yearbook editors. "In a sport marked for its non-observance of the Marquis of Queensbury's rules, he has conducted himself always as a gentleman."

Foley had always been known for his effective, but gentlemanly style of play when he was a varsity skater at the Heights. A *Boston Transcript* sportswriter noted in a run-on sentence, "He never loafs, never quits, never stalls; because he loves to play hockey, plays clean, and never puts personal glory above team play; because he takes his bumps with a smile, keeps calm, cool and collected; because he is aggressive, talented, courageous, canny—and all despite the fact that he is a veritable midget in size."

Foley, who skated at McHugh Forum on the BC campus until a week before he died in 1983, was the only three-sport letterman in his graduating class, having played four years of varsity hockey, four of basketball, and two of football. In hockey, he presaged the arrival, some eight decades later, of Brian Gionta, Nathan Gerbe, and Johnny Gaudreau.

BC's 1928 Ice Hockey Tea—with coach James "Sonny" Foley in front row, center, and future head coach John "Snooks" Kelley, front row, far right. (*Photo courtesy of Boston College Sports Media Relations*)

Even back in the 1920s the Eagles were a team with a place for a good "little" man.

The Roaring Twenties—yes, indeed. And Boston College hockey was right there in the thick of it until March 1, 1929. The Eagles ended the season with a 6-1 triumph over Holy Cross. It would be their last game until February 1933, as the stock market crash in October ushered in the Great Depression. The *Boston Globe*'s coverage of that final contest complimented Arthur Morrissey, a "veteran defense man who was brilliant, not only on defense but also in attacking, but for his willingness to pass to team-mates, his individual scoring record was not affected."

BOSTON COLLEGE'S FIRST WORLD CHAMPION: PETE SANFORD

Sophomore Lawrence "Pete" Sanford scored two of the goals in Boston College's final game of 1929. He graduated in 1932, the year before hockey was reinstituted, so he never played another game for Boston College. But his play on the international scene, after the stock market crash and the

Great Depression's onset curtailed BC hockey, made Sanford the Eagles' first World Champion hockey player.

When the Boston Olympics defeated the Montreal Junior Canadiens 5-4 at the Boston Garden one day in the early '30s, a reporter called it the "rip-roaringest amateur hockey game Boston ice has ever known since the collapse of the old 'cigar box' league." The Olympics rallied from a 4-0 deficit to tie the game, with Sanford scoring the third goal and assisting on the winner.

The reporter wrote of Sanford: "famous right wing on the best known schoolboy hockey line ever developed in Greater Boston, looked like the Melrose star of 1923–24–25 in the final period when he skated through the Canadiens and flipped a pass to Bob Nelson for the winning goal at 10:31."

Sanford would have graduated in 1931, but he took a semester off to play for coach Walter Brown's United States team in the World Amateur Tournament in Krynica, Poland. The Americans lost the championship to Canada 2-0. A writeup sent back to America by an unnamed local correspondent called the game, "The Great Encounter . . . it was a fight as seldom seen by a European . . . one could hear the hockey sticks crashing together, sometimes breaking from the force of the opposing puck . . . the Canadians showed better technique, while the Americans showed more fight and sometimes were faster in skating."

That wasn't the end of Sanford's 1931 hockey adventures. The Americans toured several European countries after the tournament. In Berlin, they defeated the Berlin Skating Club 4-1. *New York Evening Post* Foreign Service Correspondent H. R. Knickerbocker called it "a medium for the expression in international prejudices when 6000 German spectators ripped out the brass railings at the Sports Palast and threatened violence to America's star amateur team, the Boston Hockey Club."

In 1931–32, Sanford could have been Boston College hockey's first US Olympian. It didn't happen. As a Boston paper reported, "Coach Alfred Winsor, coach of the United States Olympic hockey team, yesterday was obliged to rearrange the list of players he will take to Lake Placid on Saturday . . . he had expected to take as one of his three right wings Pete Sanford of Boston College . . . but it developed yesterday that Sanford, who is a senior at college this year, has been unable to get permission from the

Boston College regent to make the trip, which would demand several weeks' absence from classes."

Just three weeks after Boston College varsity hockey resumed under Snooks Kelley and Bill Hogan Jr., Pete Sanford drank from the World Championship trophy. He was in Prague with the Massachusetts Rangers, the team assembled by Walter Brown for a barnstorming tour of Europe and another go at the title.

Lawrence Sanford was kept out of the 1932 Olympics by school officials who thought he would miss too many classes while competing. (*Photo courtesy of the Brown family*)

This time they succeeded. On February 24, 1933, in the tournament's final game before a crowd of twelve thousand, the Americans edged Canada 2-1 in overtime. It was the first time the Canadians, coached by Toronto Maple Leafs roguish future owner Harold Ballard, had ever lost to any nation in international competition. America would not win another gold medal until the Squaw Valley Olympics in 1960. All of America's wins, other than the final, were shutouts. Sanford played right wing on the second line and scored one goal.

THE RESURRECTION OF BC HOCKEY

The sport of ice hockey at Boston College— as we know it today—would not exist without the efforts of William M. Hogan Jr. '33. Bill Hogan, a native of Cambridge, Massachusetts, was instrumental in resurrecting this treasured sport at Boston College, following the suspension of hockey as a varsity sport during the Great Depression. "BC almost went out of business," Hogan explained in an interview shortly before his death in 2012.

Although several former hockey studentathletes banded together to play in local amateur leagues (a team being known as "*Boston Combinations*"), inter-collegiate competition was not available.

"I went to BC expecting to play hockey," Hogan said. "I was very disappointed when they dropped the sport. A lot of high school players from the area were actually going up to Dartmouth to play, because Dartmouth had ice all the time in the winter." The only indoor ice facility in Boston at the time was the Boston Arena.

As president of his class and an avid hockey player, Hogan campaigned to reestablish the sport at the Heights—enlisting the support of the Boston College senior administration and of Athletics Director John P. Curley. He even arranged practice time for a BC team at the Arena, where he was able to convince General Manager George Brown to donate several early-morning hours per week to the proposed team.

The school eventually agreed to provide limited financial support. The new team was given old football jerseys as team uniforms and players provided their own skates, sticks, and other equipment. Hogan even persuaded his old Cambridge friend and former BC hockey player John "Snooks" Kelley '28 to become the volunteer coach of the new team.

When the team gathered at Boston Arena for its first varsity game—against Northeastern—the players unanimously voted Hogan as team captain in recognition of his great efforts. BC won that game, 8-6, and went on to a 3-2-1 record in that first year of hockey renewal. Hogan proved to be as valuable on the ice as off, scoring both goals in a 2-1 victory over MIT, and single goals against Boston University and Brown in that abbreviated season. He finished with eight points in his brief varsity career—and tied for the team's leading point total in the 1932–33 season.

Hogan went on to earn a law degree from Harvard, but never forgot his ties to his alma mater, serving on both the Alumni Association and Athletic Association Boards for many years. His son, Bill Hogan III, earned All-America honors as an Eagle hockey player in 1962.

Bill Hogan Jr. was born in April 1912—in the same week that the new Fenway Park opened in Boston and the great steamship *Titanic* struck an iceberg and sank on its maiden voyage across the Atlantic Ocean. Bill passed away at age 100, several months after throwing out the first pitch during a ceremony in Fenway Park in the spring of 2012.

3

SNOOKS
The "Dean" of American College Hockey Coaches

Sitting at his cluttered desk deep inside the McHugh Forum hockey rink on a late January day in 1970, John A. "Snooks" Kelley—who had guided, coached, and nurtured the Boston College hockey program since its rebirth in 1933—opened a letter from an undergraduate academic dean.

The brief communication stated that one of Kelley's key players had been placed on academic probation for failure to attend his classes in introductory business law. The university's academic regulations of the day allowed for no more than six unexcused absences per semester, and the player had far exceeded his limit. He was ruled ineligible to participate in that Friday's game against a red-hot Colgate team, as well as upcoming contests against archrival Boston University and the first round of the annual Beanpot Tournament.

Kelley quickly donned his trademark black overcoat and matching fedora—he already had on a pair of oversized rubber galoshes that he wore every day in the cold rink—and headed up campus to Fulton Hall to meet with his player's teacher, Frank J. Parker, S.J., a young Jesuit Scholastic in the final stages of spiritual preparation before being ordained to the priesthood.

Arriving at the faculty offices on Fulton's third floor, Kelley announced to the receptionist: "My name is John Kelley. I coach the Boston College hockey team, and I need to see Father Parker right away. It's an emergency."

"You can go right in," the secretary said, pointing to a small office at the end of the corridor. "But I should tell you that he is still a Jesuit Scholastic and should be referred to as '*Mister Parker*.'"

Lowering his booming voice to a loud stage whisper, "Snooks" replied, "I know that, dear," using the affectionate term for any female whose name he did not know. "But all the young guys like to be called '*Father*.'"

Once inside the fledgling teacher's office, Kelley dropped to his knees, clasped his hands in front of him, and begged for academic mercy for both his truant player and the future well-being of the BC hockey program. "Father, Mr. Flynn [Athletics Director Bill Flynn] told me that he would fire me if I had four losses this year," the coach pleaded. "I've already got three." Both men knew that Flynn would never have issued such an ultimatum.

"But [the player] hasn't been showing up to class," countered Parker. "He *will* attend class, Father," Kelley promised.

"He doesn't even have the book," argued Parker. "He *will* get the book, Father," pleaded Kelley. "And, he *will* read it."

Equally impressed by his visitor's earnestness and his blarney, Parker agreed to allow the would-be student-athlete another chance. Kelley was delighted.

On the way out, the receptionist—knowing full well the purpose of Kelley's visit—asked him how he had made out in the meeting. "A piece of cake, dear." He winked. "A piece of cake.

"Now, can you tell me where I can find the English department?"

* * *

A master recruiter, a strong motivator, and an intensely loyal alumnus, Snooks Kelley won 501 games in 36 seasons as head coach of the Boston College Eagles—the most victories of any college coach up to that time. He did it as a part-time mentor who taught school in Cambridge before heading over to the campus rink or other facilities that were homes for his team's practices or games over the years.

"He would have made a wonderful politician," says former BC hockey star Sherm Saltmarsh '53, who himself served seven terms in the Massachusetts State Legislature, representing his hometown of Winchester. "Snooks had such a strong affection for Boston College. He also kept a positive approach. He created a bond with his players and with their families. He was the most sincere person I ever met."

Kelley never referred to his alma mater as "BC." He always used the full "Boston College" in speaking of the institution he so loved.

John A. "Snooks" Kelley—the "Dean" of American College Hockey Coaches (*Photo courtesy of Boston College Sports Media Relations*)

*   *   *

Boston College's longest-serving hockey coach (1932–1972, with four years spent in military service during World War II), John Andrew Kelley was born in Cambridge, Massachusetts, on July 11, 1907, the only son of Daniel and Mary Kelley, natives of Kilkenney, Ireland, who, like tens of thousands of others, emigrated to the greater Boston area from their native land. To Kelley's older sisters, the toddler who had clearly inherited his parents' Irish facial features resembled "Baby Snookums"—an infant character in the popular comic strip *The Newlyweds* that featured a young couple and their chubby-faced baby. The character's name was shortened to "Baby Snooks" over the years, and young John Kelley had a nickname that would last him for the rest of his life.

John Kelley, who grew up at 129 Raymond St. in North Cambridge, never participated in organized hockey as a youngster, although he and his friends loved to play the game at nearby "Jerry's Pit"—a small quarry that when frozen over made an ideal site for a neighborhood pick-up contest. He attended Boston College High School—then located off Harrison Avenue in the South End of Boston—but didn't play hockey. After graduation, he joined many of his BC High classmates in enrolling at Boston College in Chestnut Hill, where he quickly signed up to become a manager for the school's hockey team.

As manager, Snooks would often put on skates during practice to facilitate his duties. Eagles' coach Fred Rocque stressed a short, precise passing game for his team, and occasionally, he would ask young Kelley to help out on the ice by passing the puck to teammates who were practicing a specific maneuver.

In Kelley's senior season he was named head manager and was reacquainted with an old Cambridge friend, James "Sonny" Foley '25, who had been a star player for BC as an undergraduate and in 1927 succeeded Rocque as the Eagles' head coach. During a New Year's Eve game against Yale at Boston Arena, BC center Larry Gibson crashed into the boards and suffered a severe neck sprain and "head troubles" so serious that he was admitted to Boston's Carney Hospital for treatment.

Foley needed another player for upcoming games against Boston University and Holy Cross, so he gave a uniform to his old neighbor Snooks, who had practiced with the team as manager and had a good idea of the favored offensive strategies. That decision thrilled the five-foot-eight-inch, 156-pound. center, who went out and scored an unassisted goal against the Crusaders in his second varsity game, helping BC to a 5-4 victory.

After graduation, Kelley accepted a teaching job in the Cambridge Public School system, joining the faculty at Haggarty Junior High School, and coaching amateur teams in the area, including the Cambridge Red Sox, a baseball club in the Suburban Twilight League, and the Cantab Cubs, a local hockey team that won the Bay State Amateur League championship with Kelley behind the bench.

At the end of the 1928–29 season, Boston College dropped its varsity hockey program in the face of mounting financial difficulties caused almost entirely by the Great Depression. Rev. James H. Dolan, S.J., the president of Boston College, had to cut back on athletic expenditures to try to balance the loss of tuition income and a marked increase in financial aid that had been forced by the nation's economic woes.

When William M. Hogan Jr. '33—the senior class president who possessed the great attributes of oratorical skill, charismatic leadership, and hockey-playing ability—persuaded Fr. Dolan's successor, Rev. Louis J. Gallagher, S.J., to reinstate ice hockey as a varsity sport, he also suggested that the college bring back his old Cambridge colleague— John "Snooks" Kelley—to coach the new team.

Kelley returned to the Heights as a volunteer coach. A legendary coaching career was launched. A new era in Boston College sports history was about to begin.

* * *

Kelley's introduction to his new team came at 6 a.m. on Friday, January 13, 1933, when seventy candidates turned out to compete for spots on the Eagles' varsity roster. Practices were held early in the day—sometimes as early as 3 a.m. but the team was grateful to have the free ice time. For years, the team was dubbed "the Milkmen" in reference to their early-morning practice slots.

Fifteen days after the initial tryouts were called, the Boston College Eagles beat Northeastern 8-6 and Kelley had his first coaching victory.

Hogan, who had shown such persistence in reincarnating the BC hockey program, was unanimously chosen as team captain. Ray Funchion, a rushing defenseman from Danvers and St. John's Prep, scored four goals in that milestone game. The rookie coach also put together BC's first big line of the hockey revival: teaming up center Hogan with right wing Herb Crimlisk and left wing Frank "Kiddo" Liddell—all Cambridge residents— on the same wave.

Kelley's first team ended the year with a 3-2-1 record.

BC's teams gradually began to improve, although the 1933–34 unit slipped to 2-6-1 (only one of four losing campaigns that Kelley would endure in his lengthy career). Funchion was team captain in 1934, but had his season curtailed in a February 4 game against the St. Dominique Hockey Club, an amateur outfit in Lewiston, Maine. Funchion, who ordinarily wore a football helmet in games because of a skull fracture suffered playing the fall sport, took the leather headgear off because of the heat in the arena and was promptly clubbed by an opponent. He spent the next week in the hospital and did not return to play that season.

In 1935, Kelley's Eagles scored a monumental 3-2 overtime victory over Dartmouth in a game played before 1,500 fans at the Arena. Dartmouth was considered college hockey's top program (the NCAA championship tournament would not be initiated for another twelve years). Defenseman Joe Walsh contributed two of the goals—one of them the game-winner— Funchion added another, and goaltender Tim Ready played a strong game, shutting down the powerful Dartmouth attack after surrendering a pair of first period scores.

Coach John "Snooks" Kelley and members of the 1935–36 team—Peter Murphy, Tim Ready, Jack Burgess, captain Fred Moore, Dick McDonald, and Joe Walsh. (*Photo courtesy of Boston College University Archives*)

Later that year, Ready, who like almost all goaltenders of the day did not wear a mask or helmet, was knocked unconscious when a hard shot hit his head in a game against archrival Boston University. Out cold for ten minutes, Ready also suffered a deep gash on his forehead and a swollen eye. He returned to finish the game, beating the Terriers, 2-1, for BC's first victory in the city rivalry since 1928.

Ready continued to prove himself to be a top-shelf goaltender again the following season, stopping an amazing 82 saves—a record that still stands today—in a 1-1 tie at Princeton. Nineteen of the stops came in the ten-minute overtime frame.

By 1937, college hockey was becoming formalized with the institution of the New England Intercollegiate Hockey League that included Boston College, Boston University, Northeastern, MIT, University of New Hampshire, Colby, and Middlebury—a forerunner of the eventual ECAC alignment. BC won the first league title with a 5-1-1 record in league play (8-4-1 overall.)

Along with the formation of a new league and the solid foundation of Eagle hockey, Kelley was awarded a small annual stipend. It was not enough to allow him to give up his teaching job, although he eventually stepped down as assistant headmaster at Haggarty School and switched to Cambridge Latin School, where he taught history and had a more flexible schedule. While a part-time coach for more than three decades, Kelley never realized more than $3,000 a year from Boston College as his coaching salary.

* * *

The Eagles played on a bigger hockey stage in the 1940 season after Kelley had enticed another Cambridge star, Ray Chaisson, the son of French-Canadian parents, to join his team. Kelley placed Chaisson in the center ice position, with Johnny Pryor and Elphege "Fishy" Dumont on the wings, and the trio became the highest-scoring line in college hockey. Chaisson alone had 67 points (33 goals, 34 assists) in the 1939–40 season, and the 12-5-1 Eagles won a New England title. The 1940–41 club was even better, finishing 13-1 and winning the regional crown again, as Chaisson averaged a shade over four points a game.

Chaisson, Dumond, and teammate Bob Mee were offered a chance to play for a Boston Bruins minor league team, the Boston Olympics, and the three grabbed the opportunity, figuring that they were soon headed into military service. The draft was delayed that year, but the brief excursion into professional hockey cost each of them their eligibility, and their BC careers were prematurely finished.

Unfazed by the loss of some of his top players, Kelley just reloaded—piloting his 1941–42 club to a 12-2 season record—losing only to traditional powerhouses Princeton and Dartmouth. Glowing with success, Boston College entered the Amateur Athletic Union national championship tournament at the end of the college campaign and swept to an American championship with a thrilling 9-8 victory over the Massena (New York) Hockey Club in a game that saw the Eagles tie the score at 8-all on Wally Boudreau's goal with just 20 seconds left in regulation and then winning, 9-8, in overtime on a goal scored by Harry Crovo.

After the season, Kelley would head off to the service himself, serving as a physical education instructor in the Navy and preparing naval aviation cadets for the rigors of flight training at bases in Illinois, Iowa, and North Carolina. One of his fellow instructors was Bud Wilkinson, later a Hall of Fame football coach at the University of Oklahoma, and the two remained close friends throughout their lives. Kelley rose to the rank of lieutenant commander before being mustered out of service after the war and heading back to Boston to resume his teaching and coaching vocations.

* * *

While Kelley and a large part of BC's student population were serving the country during World War II, the hockey program was kept going through the efforts of a couple of volunteers, including Johnny Temple—the BC baseball coach who agreed to take over hockey duties in 1942–43—and Rev. Joseph Glavin, S.J., a philosophy teacher who loved the sport and offered to help keep the team going with a watered-down three-game schedule in 1945–46 until Kelley returned. With a student body minimized by military commitments and with a decision not to allow resident army training cadets to play sports, the university did not field a varsity hockey team in 1944–45.

After the war and thanks in part to the GI Bill, tens of thousands of returning military veterans were able to enroll in the nation's college and universities. As Snooks soon found out, some of them were pretty good hockey players, and they were headed to Chestnut Hill. The Boston College teams of the late 1940s would put the Eagles on top of the college hockey world.

*   *   *

Giles Threadgold of Newton, who earned two Purple Heart medals for injuries he received in Italy and during the Battle of the Bulge while serving in Europe with the army's famed 82nd Airborne Division, was one of the war-tested veterans to don BC's maroon and gold. After surgery on his spine and eye, Threadgold, who had grown up skating on the Charles River before becoming a paratrooper, was told that he would likely never be able to participate in strenuous physical activities again.

He laughed at the prognosis.

"I came back from the service," he said from his home on Cape Cod in 2013, "and went out for the BC team, along with about a hundred others. I thought I had done well in the tryouts, but when they posted the names of those who made the team, my name was not there. The next night, I went in to see my aunt who worked for Walter Brown, the president of the Boston Garden. Just as I arrived, Snooks Kelley also came through the door into Walter's office. Walter said, 'Snooks, I have a good guy for you,' and Snooks, who was never without a good line, replied, 'Oh, I know, I am going to take good care of him.' Walter got called away and Snooks leaned over to me and said, "Kid, what's your name?' [laughter] and told me to report the next day to get a uniform. That's how I made the team at BC."

It was a good choice for Kelley. Threadgold was a fleet and fearless skater who could defend and harass the top scorer on any opposing team. As an irascible team prankster as well, the wiry Threadgold was the perfect addition to Kelley's postwar clubs that featured strong scorers, rugged defensemen, and solid goaltenders.

"I was one of the very few kids who went to BC right out of high school," noted Warren Lewis, an Arlington native who had attended

Boston College High School. "All of the others were coming back from military service. Some of them were twenty-five or twenty-six years old."

Lewis, another fleet skater, made the varsity squad as a freshman and wound up leading the team in scoring in the 1946–47 season with 23 goals and 43 total points as the Eagles soared to a 15-3-1 record. He was joined on the line by Jimmy Fitzgerald, another direct admit from Wellesley High who had been deferred from military service by a slight heart murmur. Lewis, Fitzgerald, Bob Mason, and Jack Mulhern provided all of the firepower the team needed to make their mark on the national stage.

All-America honoree Ed "Butch" Songin, a rangy Walpole, Massachusetts, native who remains as one of the finest athletes ever to compete for the Eagles, led the way defensively. The big defenseman routinely played a full 60 minutes in each game. Songin also quarterbacked the BC football team and later became a starting signal-caller in both the Canadian Football League and for the original Boston Patriots of the new American Football League. Bernie Burke, a Newton native who spent a year at BC before enlisting as a Navy medic and seeing action in several of the major amphibious invasions of World War II, returned to campus to handle goaltending duties.

With a 12-4 regular season record, Boston College qualified for the New England playoffs, the first step in competing for the national title. BC scored an impressive 10-1 victory over Bowdoin, and then played Northeastern for the NCAA bid.

The day before the game against Northeastern, the impish Threadgold had obtained the home phone numbers of four of the Huskies' players. Setting his alarm for 4 a.m., Threadgold called the NU players in the middle of the night, saying to each, "This is Giles Threadgold from BC, and we are playing you tonight. Why don't you just stay home, because we are going to whip your ass." The brazen prank caused chaos among the Northeastern players. "They all wanted to kill me," Threadgold said with glee.

Instead, that night, while the Huskies futilely chased the elusive Threadgold all over the ice to extract revenge, the rest of the BC players took target practice on the NU goal, and the Eagles skated to a 6-4 win and a ticket to Colorado to compete with Dartmouth, the University of Michigan, and the hometown favorite, Colorado College.

* * *

Building on the Eagles' success in the national competition, Kelley was able to recruit the very best skaters in the Boston area. Saltmarsh, for example, was a top player at Winchester High School before deciding to spend a postgraduate year at Vermont's Kimball Union Academy in preparation for his expected matriculation at Dartmouth.

Midway through his postgrad year, Saltmarsh decided that he wanted to attend a college closer to his home. He went over to Boston College, where he joined other candidates taking an entrance examination administered in the classrooms of the school's trademark Tower Building—not yet named Gasson Hall.

"We wrote our answers in a bluebook, and they corrected them while we waited," Saltmarsh said. "Later, I met with Coach Kelley right out on the Tower Building lawn and told him that I was at Kimball Union and wanted to go to BC. He said, 'Son, what is that?' At the time, everybody who went to BC to play hockey lived right in the shadows of the campus.

"He said to me, 'Well, son, I have already given out twenty-two scholarships to the incoming freshman class, but I will give you the same opportunity as everybody else.'"

Jim Fitzgerald, who had been the offensive star of the NCAA championship tournament, was the new freshman coach, and he

Sherm Saltmarsh, center, is flanked by two other stars of the early 1950s—goaltender Peter Maggio and forward Wellington "Wimpy" Burtnett. (*Photo courtesy of Boston College Sports Media Relations*)

25

started weeding through the seventy candidates who tried out for freshman hockey in the fall of 1949. "A lot of guys who had scholarships were cut. But what a team it was—we never lost a game," Saltmarsh said. He was the squad's leading scorer.

The demands on student-athletes were far less in the early 1950s than could ever be imagined today. The Boston College team, which still did not have an on-campus rink, practiced three or four times per week—rarely more than an hour at a time. During the Christmas season, Saltmarsh held a job in the Winchester Post Office, and with his postmaster's blessing, would leave his job at 4:30 p.m. to attend a 5:30 practice session. He would be back sorting mail by 7. Still without a scholarship, he had to save his earnings for BC's $400 yearly tuition.

The Boston College teams of the era continued to excel in New England competition, but struggled in national NCAA play, losing first-round and consolation games in postseason play in both 1954 and 1956. Three of those four losses came at the hands of Western opponents.

* * *

The 1951 season featured one of the wildest comebacks in Eagle hockey history: Down 9-5 to Harvard in the third period of a game played at the Boston Arena on February 5, BC scored five consecutive goals to win the game, 10-9, in regulation. With the score tied 9-9 and just over two minutes left on the clock, sophomore Joe Morgan—like Ceglarski and Songin, a talented Walpole product—begged Kelley to put him on the ice to take a faceoff in the Harvard zone. Snooks agreed with his young player—who years later would become the manager of the Boston Red Sox—and Morgan pulled the dropped puck back to Ceglarski, who fired it home for the winner.

* * *

Kelley, as a part-time coach and full-time teacher, never really developed the sophisticated and technical approach to the game that modern coaches now employ. His practices were devoted primarily to conditioning and

Len Ceglarski was an All-America wing for the Eagles in his playing days. (*Photo courtesy of Boston College Sports Media Relations*)

basic plays. His principal strategy was to have his defensemen fire the puck up the ice, where his always-talented forwards would have a chance to make something happen. He rarely worked on a power play or penalty killing in his limited practice time—figuring he would send his best players out on the ice in a special-teams situation. "We would shoot the puck into the zone and skate like hell to keep it there," recalled Threadgold. "We got five men into the offensive zone. That was all Snooks wanted to do."

"He was a very basic hockey man," added Saltmarsh. "We never did anything fancy. He depended a lot on his players' natural ability. But he did have a knack for putting the right people together, creating a chemistry."

Billy Hogan III, the son of the man who had helped resurrect Boston College hockey and bring Kelley behind the Eagles' dasher, recalls the standard practice sessions of the day: loosening up period; skating drills and stops-and-starts; skating at full speed around and around the rink, then reversing direction and doing it again; 3-on-2 and 2-on-1 drills; followed by another fifteen minutes of hard skating.

"He was always creating the thought process that you always had *more* skating to do," Hogan said. "Like in the third period of a game. It was mental as well as physical. I can tell you, those were really hard practices, but it made a big difference when we were in a high-pressure game."

Sometimes, Snooks's hard-skating practices drew the ire of rink maintenance personnel, who recoiled at the sight of their surfaces being chewed up by the constant stops and starts involved. "We were playing in a Christmas tournament in St. Louis in 1971 at the old Checkerdome," recalled Tom Mellor, an All-America defenseman who also played on the US Olympic hockey team that captured a silver medal at Sapporo in 1972. "After we finished our practice, Snooks had this drill called 'the Pack,' where the team would gather behind one of the goals—both of which had been pulled out. He would place a fast skater out at the red line and would say, 'Now catch him—twenty laps!' and blow the whistle to start. Off we would go, circling and circling and circling. It was a great conditioning drill. All of a sudden, the guy who took care of the ice in the building ran out and started going crazy. The ice was all cut up—and the Blues had a game that night. He kept yelling, 'What the hell is this guy doing?'"

* * *

No one worked harder in Kelley's exhausting practices than John Cunniff, a young man who grew up in a poor family living in a three-decker home on East 2nd Street of South Boston. "You never had to motivate John," said his brother Ted of the two-time collegiate All-America player who was BC's all-time leading scorer (151 points in 75 games) in his three-year varsity career (1963–66) and later became an Olympian, professional player, and NHL head coach.

As a youngster, Cunniff never had the advantage of playing organized hockey, but would never pass up the opportunity to improve his skills by playing in the one of the frequent pick-up games going on in Southie's playground rinks.

Cunniff, whose family could not afford skates until he was a teenager, worked tirelessly with ankle weights and body weights and even practiced shooting a weighted puck to build up his endurance and skill. His mother insisted that he go to Boston's Don Bosco Trade School to learn a work skill, but when he realized that he might have a future in college hockey, Cunniff took a postgraduate year at New Prep in Cambridge, a school that not only sharpened students' academic skills, but produced dozens of Division I hockey players. He came to BC without benefit of a hockey scholarship, but that situation did not last long when Kelley realized the immense skills and work ethic of his new recruit.

John Cunniff—one of BC's greatest (*Photo courtesy of Boston College Sports Media Relations*)

Cunniff was assigned to a line with crafty center Phil Dyer of Melrose and Rhode Island product Jim Mullen, another goal-scoring sniper. The trio became known as the "Production Line" for their steady offensive output, but Cunniff was the definite leader.

"He could change speeds like no one else," said linemate Mullen. "If he saw an opening, no one could catch him."

Cunniff was especially impressive in the Beanpot Tournament spotlight. The Eagles won rare back-to-back championships in 1964 and 1965, as the quiet man from Southie tallied four goals and nine points in the two tournaments.

Following the 1964–65 regular season, the Eagles advanced to the ECAC championship with consecutive playoff victories over Dartmouth, Clarkson, and Brown. The championship earned BC a slot in the NCAA Championship tournament held at the new Meehan Arena at Brown. "I was the only non-Massachusetts kid on the team," recalled Mullen, who was from nearby Warwick, Rhode Island. "When I came to BC, I had dreams of playing for a national championship in Minnesota or Denver. Where did I get to go? The city where I was born."

With the powerful scoring line of Cunniff-Dyer-Mullen, the top scoring line in all of college hockey that year, and some acrobatic goaltending by Pat Murphy, a superb athlete from Wellesley, Massachusetts, the Eagles were ready for the semifinal game against North Dakota. The star of BC's 4-3 victory that night, however, was a young sophomore center who not only showed a nice scoring touch on his two goals, but the leadership skills that would eventually carry him to an even loftier place in the college hockey profession: Jerry York.

In the championship game played on March 20, the Eagles were stonewalled by Michigan Tech, 8-2, a team lead by their talented goaltender, future Chicago Blackhawk and Hockey Hall of Famer Tony Esposito.

As a senior, Cunniff was sidelined when blindsided by a vicious hit from Brown's rugged forward Dennis Macks. The collision separated Cunniff's shoulder and put him on the bench for eight games—and nearly ignited a riot in the packed McHugh Forum that night, as Eagle hockey fans were horrified at the mayhem inflicted on their star player by the rough-and-tumble Macks.

Cunniff continued his impressive hockey accomplishments long after graduating from the Heights. He was a member of the 1968 US Olympic Team that competed in Grenoble, France, and later played professional hockey for the WHA's New England Whalers. A great student of the game as well, he twice assisted Herb Brooks on the Team USA coaching staff (in 1998 and 2002) and was head coach of the New Jersey Devils from 1989–1991. He died from cancer at age fifty-seven in 2002. His Boston College sweater is retired and hangs in a place of honor in the Conte Forum rafters.

BC Athletics Director Bill Flynn is joined by Marge Kelley and daughter Candy in the dedication of the Kelley Rink in Conte Forum in her late husband's honor. (*Photo courtesy of Boston College Sports Media Relations*)

* * *

After Cunniff departed, the scoring mantle fell to newly elected team captain York, who earned All-America honors for his sparkling play at center in BC's 18-7 regular season finish in 1966–67. The Eagles clocked Ceglarski's Clarkson team 9-2 in the first round of the ECAC Tournament, but in turn were buried, 12-2, by Cornell and their sensational goaltender, Ken Dryden, in the league semifinals played at Boston Garden. Dryden, a rare three-time All-America selection, would prove to be a nemesis for the Eagles as long as he suited up for Coach Ned Harkness' Cornell national champions.

A year later, BC posted a 17-9 regular season mark and ignited in the ECAC playoffs again—tipping St. Lawrence, 7-6, and Clarkson,

6-5—both in thrilling overtime games to win the right to meet Cornell again for the Eastern championship. Dryden paced the Big Red to a 6-3 victory in that one, but the Eagles had played well enough to draw an invitation to the NCAA tournament in frigid Duluth, Minnesota. There they lost to the WCHA's Denver Pioneers and had to face Cornell once again in the consolation game to end the season. Dryden and his mates beat BC for the third time that year, this time by a 6-1 count.

*   *   *

Always a gentleman who exhibited great sportsmanship and love for the game, Kelley abhorred fighting or overly rough play. He never used profane language, rarely coming out with anything stronger than a loud *"goldarnit"* when something went wrong on the ice.

Kelley was a great friend and mentor to his players as well. He socialized with the players and their families after every game. His wife, Marge, often accompanied him on road trips, and the two would spend hours conversing with the student-athletes about their families, their lives, and their goals. After players graduated, he would frequently attend their weddings and other family events. Snooks often hosted former players and their families at summer cottages that he and his family rented at Pigeon Cove in Gloucester and the Humarock Beach section of Scituate.

Two weeks after Jim Mullen arrived as a freshman in 1962, his father, a well-known high school hockey coach in Rhode Island, suddenly passed away. Kelley summoned the heartbroken young man to McHugh Forum and sat with him in the bleachers, gently talking him through his pain. "You have my condolences on the loss of your dad," he told the young freshman who had yet to step onto the Boston College ice. "But now, you are part of our family too, and I will be here for you." Mullen was deeply moved by the gesture. "It was a beautiful thing for him to do for me," he said.

Hockey has always been a game replete with injuries—most of them not serious. During freshman tryouts in 1949, however, one young hopeful fell and hit the blade of another player's skate. The injured player, Robert "Jake" Boudreau, lost an eye. Kelley encouraged Boston College alumni and friends to rally to the young man's aid, putting together a massive fundraiser in Boudreau's hometown of Cambridge to help defray treatment expenses. Kelley was joined at the head table by BC football coach Denny Myers, Eagle basketball coach Gen. Al McClellan, National League baseball umpire Artie Gore, and a host of other political figures and sports luminaries to generate funds for the injured freshman.

* * *

For all of his many good attributes, Kelley did have one bad habit: like many Americans of his day, he was a cigarette smoker, even sometimes lighting up in the locker room as he was addressing the team between periods. In later years, he did not often don skates and go out on the ice, preferring to direct practice from the relative comfort of the team bench. But Ceglarski remembers that when he did have his skates on, he was unable to snuff out his still-smoldering cigarette butts, so he would have to loudly summon a manager to come over and crush the still-burning remains.

The smoking may have contributed to frequent bouts of bronchitis—and the cold hockey rinks did nothing to alleviate the condition. He rarely missed a practice or game in his 36 years of coaching, however. Likewise, even when returning from long road trips—sometimes reaching his Waban home as late as 2 or 3 a.m.—he never failed to be at his homeroom desk when the first bell rang at Cambridge Latin High the next morning.

* * *

No story about the legacy of Snooks Kelley would be complete without reference to his inspiring pregame and intermission pep talks. He would always start his pregame remarks by stating: "As you are making your last-minute preparations. . . ." And then urge his charges to try to win the night's game for their parents, siblings, school, country, or whatever else might pop into his mind.

Len Ceglarski, a key player on the 1949 NCAA championship team, captain of the 1950–51 Eagle squad, and, eventually, the coaching successor to Snooks, remembers a 1949 game against American International

College, a school that had just launched its hockey program and had lost to the Eagles, 10-2, earlier in the season.

"It was a terrible night outside and we had about sixteen people in the stands. Snooks started by saying, 'Well, gang, as far as I am concerned, this is the most important game on our schedule.' At that time, Butch Songin piped in and said, 'For Chrissake, Coach. . . .' Everyone laughed."

Mullen recalls that Snooks would become particularly loquacious when the Eagles played Harvard. "He was the Knute Rockne of hockey," he said. "Before one Harvard game, he said, 'Boys, when you skate around the rink tonight, I want you to look up at the stands. You're going to see all those Harvard Protestants up there; you'll see them with their camel hair jackets and their flashy ties, and with their flashy women beside them. They have no idea what life is about! Now, I want you to think about your own poor mothers and fathers—the poor Irish who can't even rub two nickels together.'"

Kelley, of course, did not care that all of his players were not of Irish heritage or even practicing Catholics, nor did he acknowledge that many Boston College alumni had their own important and well-paying jobs, purchased their clothing at Brooks Brothers, or—like Snooks himself—had married beautiful women.

"He would talk about work ethic and integrity, and he would just go on and on," Mullen said. "But, whenever we played Harvard, he would bring that same story up. It still makes me laugh today."

One night, a puck went flying out over the rink glass in McHugh Forum and struck a woman over her eye. She was brought immediately into the BC training room to have the wound treated by the team doctor. A few minutes later, Snooks entered the adjoining locker room and began one of his famous intermission speeches, urging his charges to rise up against the night's opponent who at the time held a narrow lead over the Eagles.

When the doctor finished attending to the woman, he asked her if she would like to lie down on the trainer's table until her head fully cleared. "Oh no," she said. "After hearing that, I've got to get back out there and see what happens!"

SNOOKERISMS

Any player who suited up for one of John "Snooks" Kelley's teams at Boston College had his favorite list of clichés and malapropisms used by BC's legendary coach.

Here are a few of the most popular "Snookerisms" that were mentioned during the collection of interviews for this publication:

"There's many a slip 'twixt cup and lip . . ." Kelley's words to his team when the Eagles were favored in a game.

"Caught between the devil and the deep blue sea . . ." His words when the Eagles were underdogs.

"One snowflake does not a blizzard make . . ." After the team had won a big game, but had other key contests ahead.

"Henderson Pump" and *"East Overshoe"* Kelley's names for the hometowns of any BC players who were not from the Greater Boston area.

"How are your wonderful parents?" Kelley's query when seeing present or former players.

"He's a real corker . . ." Kelley's description of a student-athlete who made a big play.

"A human dynamo . . ." See above description.

"No finer man has walked on leather . . ." Someone he liked.

"Click, click, click . . ." His comment as the team practiced a scissors drill.

"All others . . ." During practice, he would call "First line out . . . second line out . . . third line out . . . all others." Players promoted onto a higher group would refer to themselves as "All others alumni."

"Not important, son. You're so good you could play with a tree branch." Response to any player who requested to play with any stick other than a Lie 7, Neutral, 4-pound. Northland Pro model that had been "curing" in the equipment room for three or more years.

"Hi'ya kid . . ." His greeting to any male whose name he did not know.

"How are you, dear . . ." His greeting to any female.

*   *   *

When Kelley became head hockey coach at Boston College, virtually every student in the school was a commuter from within the Greater Boston environs. The majority of his players came from towns bordering the Boston College campus.

After losing to the all-Canadian University of Michigan team in the 1948 NCAA Championships, Kelley reiterated his lifelong philosophy of recruiting only American players. "I decided early that one of the things I wanted to do at Boston College was to give the American boy the chance to compete with his brother from across the border," Kelley told hockey writer extraordinaire Jack Falla in 1983. "I was never *anti*-Canadian. Actually, I was *pro*-American."

Kelley never actively recruited a Canadian player for the Boston College roster, but he got a Canadian-trained one with the addition of Norm Nelson to the team in 1961. Nelson's family had moved from New Orleans to Montreal when he was eight. "As soon as we crossed the border, they put a puck in my hand," he said. Nelson played his youth hockey in the Montreal Park System and actually became the property of the Montreal Canadiens hockey club, which had territorial rights to all players in Quebec.

Nelson's family moved to Lexington, Massachusetts, when he was eighteen, and, like many BC hopefuls, he attended New Prep, where he was spotted by the Eagles' freshman coach Bernie Burke. Burke's evaluation impressed Kelley, and the head coach offered Nelson a four-year scholarship. Nelson switched back and forth between defense and forward and never logged much playing time at BC, ending his career with a single varsity letter.

Kelley was highly-respected as a coach in the eastern Massachusetts area, where he had a growing network of former players, like Jim Fitzgerald at Cambridge Latin and Eddie Burns at hockey powerhouse Arlington High School, all of whom were more than happy to help steer talented players his way. With the addition of on-campus dormitories at Boston College in 1957 and the rapidly growing reputation of the university as a leading academic institution, Kelley gradually expanded his recruiting sphere to Rhode Island, western Massachusetts, Connecticut, and even upstate New York.

In 1964, he got an inquiry from a young hockey star at Hibbing High School in Minnesota—an ore-mining town on the Mesabi Iron Range in the northernmost part of the state. Jim Green, a talented center, had been heavily recruited by the University of Minnesota Gophers, but wanted to study theology in college. The U of M offered no such program, but the Catholic chaplain in the school's Newman Center suggested that the young hockey player look to one of the eastern Catholic hockey-playing colleges—Boston College or Providence—to match his academic as well as hockey interests. Green wrote to Kelley and the coach offered him a scholarship immediately, figuring that if he was good enough to play for the powerful Gophers, he could certainly win a place on the BC roster.

Green visited Boston College in July, accepted the scholarship offer, and enrolled in September. Although Green excelled in the classroom—he later joined the Society of Jesus for fourteen years—his style of controlled Western hockey did not fit at all with Kelley's "dump and chase" strategy.

"The approach that I grew up with centered around puck control. As you went into the offensive zone, you controlled the puck and tried to set up offensive plays," he said recently from the Native American Reservation in South Dakota where he is a language teacher today. "The Eastern style just didn't make any sense to me." Green saw limited ice time in his varsity career, but he did open the door for Boston College to recruit a platoon of skilled players from the Land of 10,000 Lakes.

Hailing from St. Paul, Mike Robertson—a great all-around athlete who played hockey, punted for the BC football team, and was a hard-hitting second baseman—was the next Minnesota student-athlete to come to Chestnut Hill, and he was soon followed by one of Kelley's greatest hockey recruiting coups, Tim Sheehy.

*　　*　　*

Tim Sheehy was the first Boston College player to be born in Canada.

His mother, Kathleen, chose to bring Tim—the fourth of nine Sheehy children—into the world at Fort Frances Hospital, just over the

Ontario border from the family home in International Falls, Minnesota. At International Falls High, Tim became a hockey legend as a freshman when he powered the team to the state finals, where they lost the coveted title by an overtime goal. Sheehy, a strong skater with a blazing shot and tons of natural hockey ability, would not accept defeat in future years, as International Falls captured three consecutive state titles, an unheard of accomplishment in that hockey-rich region.

Many Western schools recruited the young Sheehy, including the University of Minnesota, Denver University, Minnesota-Duluth, Colorado College, and Michigan Tech—all of whom promised full hockey scholarships.

In the spring of Tim's junior year of high school, his parents, Larry and Kathleen, were driving east to visit their oldest son, Terence, who was a novice at the Salesian Seminary in Goshen, New York. A devout Catholic family, the Sheehys decided to continue further east to Boston to look at Boston College, the Jesuit school with a strong hockey program, as a possible choice for Tim.

When they arrived on campus, they asked to see Coach Kelley—but since it was Patriots' Day, they were informed that he was out watching the Boston Marathon on Commonwealth Avenue and could not be immediately located. Instead, BC's sports information director, Eddie Miller, offered to take the visitors on a campus tour. When the Sheehys learned that Eddie and his wife, Patti, were also the parents of nine children, a bond was immediately created and BC went right to the top of Tim's—and his parents'—college list.

The feeling for BC grew when Tim spoke with an International Falls neighbor, Jim Amidon, who had played for Colorado College a few years earlier, and raved about the enthusiasm and hockey knowledge of the fans who had packed McHugh Forum for a game when the Tigers played in Boston in 1966.

A month after Tim's high school graduation, Snooks Kelley, accompanied by Faculty Moderator of Athletics Rev. David F. Carroll, S.J., travelled to International Falls—the longest recruiting trip in his career—to visit Tim and his family and make a final pitch for Boston College.

Tim Sheehy was a prize recruit when he was playing for International Falls (Minnesota) High School. (*Photo courtesy of Boston College Sports Media Relations*)

"Of course, the 'Snooker' had always had just American players," said Sheehy in recalling the visit. "We lived right on the riverbank—Riverside Drive—and out there in the middle of the Rainy River, 100 yards or so away . . . is Canada. So, he's standing there in our living room, looking out the picture window, and he starts to wag his index finger. He said, 'You mean, that's *Canada* over there?'" The seventeen-year old Sheehy and his family were sold. He enrolled in Boston College less than two months later. Fourteen of his International Falls teammates went on to play Division I college hockey—of those, only Sheehy and one other player, who wound up at West Point, played in the east.

Sheehy would not disappoint when he arrived at the Heights. He starred for coach Bernie Burke's freshman team, and Burke returned the favor to the Minnesota lad by inviting him to his home for dinner and a family skate on an outdoor rink in one of his neighbor's yards in Newton. Teammate Kevin Ahearn, who lived in Milton, also invited Tim to his home frequently, and Kevin's mother even took on the ultimate chore of all college moms—doing her weekend visitors' laundry.

As good as the Boston College hockey program was in those days, Sheehy did notice some differences from the hockey culture of his native Minnesota. "I broke my stick during freshman practice one day," he said. "I was using a straight Victoriaville model at the time. I took the shaft into Jack Tighe, BC's old-time equipment man, and he looked at me and said, 'Where is the other piece?' I had to go back out and find the blade before he would give me a new stick. In Minnesota—even in high school—we had all brand-new equipment—with probably a half a dozen sticks in each locker. My dad called Snooks about it, and he sent me down to Bucky Warren's sporting goods store in downtown Boston, where I was allowed to get three sticks [laughter]."

Whatever sticks he had over the years had plenty of goals in them. Sheehy smashed Cunniff's scoring record with 185 points in just 80 varsity games, earning All-America kudos in both the 1969 and 1970 seasons, and earning a spot on the '72 American Olympic Team, where his roommate in Sapporo was future Minnesota and Olympic head coach Herb Brooks.

After a pro career with the Detroit Red Wings and New England Whalers, Sheehy, who had been a finance major as an undergraduate, became a highly respected and successful player agent for NHL professionals.

*   *   *

In 1966, Athletics Director Bill Flynn had authorized Kelley to add two
additional part-time staffers—former BC All-America players Tom "Red"

All-America defenseman Tom "Red" Martin (center). (*Photo courtesy of Boston College Sports Media Relations*)

Martin and Bill Daley—who worked with the Eagles' defensive and offensive units, respectively. Burke, who was still coaching the freshman team, also tutored BC's goaltenders.

When Kelley retired from the Cambridge School system in 1970, he was appointed to a full-time post as special assistant to Flynn in addition to his long-held coaching duties at the school.

On October 11, 1971, as Boston College was preparing for another hockey season, Snooks announced his plans to step down as head hockey coach at the end of the year—ending the magical era at the university that he so loved. "One of the towers on the Heights will be missing," wrote one local *Globe* writer.

"I have made up my mind that this is my last year," the sixty-four-year-old coach said in declaring that he would be calling it quits on his coaching career. "The way college hockey is today, I think that it would be in the best interests of Boston College if I stepped down." One of the reasons behind his decision was a new NCAA ruling allowing freshmen to play on the varsity level. "A student should enter college and get his feet on the ground academically and athletically with his contemporaries," he told the Boston College *Heights*.

John A. "Snooks" Kelley contemplates a practice session from the BC bench. (*Photo courtesy of Boston College Sports Media Relations*)

"Long ago, I determined that I would leave before I had to go, before my health forced me to retire," he said to the *Boston Herald's* Kevin Mannix. "Right now, thank the good Lord, I'm in excellent physical and mental shape, but I figure I've had enough."

After the stunning 500th victory over Boston University and the 501st and final win of his career with a 6-3 decision over Army two nights later, Snooks was feted by the Pike's Peak Club, a group of former BC hockey players and fans at a gala banquet in McHugh, the scene of so many of his coaching triumphs.

Hockey coaches from all over the nation attended the gala, including Vic Heyliger, his adversary from Michigan in the NCAA Tournament at Colorado Springs nearly a quarter-century earlier. Even President Richard M. Nixon sent a congratulatory telegram, stating: "500 victories is a remarkable record for any coach, and in no sport more than hockey."

As a retirement gift, the Pike's Peak Hockey Club presented him with a green 1972 Chevrolet Impala, arranged though Paul Maguire, an alumnus who owned a local automobile dealership. Snooks treasured the vehicle, attaching a maroon "I Believe in BC" bumper sticker and driving it until he passed away fourteen years later.

Later that spring, Kelley was asked to coach Team USA in the World Hockey Championships in Romania, a token of esteem from his fellow coaches and USA Hockey, the sport's amateur governing association.

Returning to campus from abroad, he set up a small office just inside the foyer of McHugh Forum. Among his duties in following years was leadership of Boston College's National Youth Sports Program, a federally funded endeavor that brought children from some of the nation's major urban areas onto nearby college campuses for recreational activities, leadership instruction, and nutrition enhancement. Snooks grew to love the children from Boston's Roxbury, Dorchester, and Jamaica Plain neighborhoods with the same fervor that he had once shown for his BC players—and fully immersed himself in creating the maximum opportunity for the inner-city children.

During the rest of the year, he would sit outside his office, where he welcomed and kibitzed with any and all visitors to the hockey rink. His guests ranged from local deliverymen to two vice presidents of the United States—Walter Mondale and George H. W. Bush. Mondale, who was on campus on May 24, 1976, to deliver the university's commencement address, was a Minnesota native and longtime college hockey fan. He even briefly held up the day's proceedings while he and Kelley chatted about favorite teams and coaches from the Gopher State.

When Bush was introduced to Kelley at commencement exercises in 1984, he replied, "Oh, I know the coach well. As a student at Yale, I played against his team."

John A. Kelley died from cancer in Boston's Carney Hospital on April 10, 1986. His funeral Mass was celebrated in St. Ignatius Church on BC's campus. Ironically, as the funeral cortege took a final circle past McHugh Forum, the site of so many of his life's highlights, demolition equipment to take down the old building was being wheeled into place.

It was time for a new chapter in Boston College hockey.

4

THE IMPOSSIBLE DREAM

Boston College Wins a Game for the Ages

Ever since McHugh Forum opened in 1958 as the home lair of the Boston College Eagles, the BC Pep Band has carried on a musical tradition that is the unmistakable signal of victory for the school's beloved hockey team.

As the game clock winds down, and with the Eagles holding a lead—as they so often do—the band will strike up the old World War II song that is so familiar to BC hockey fans, "The Beer Barrel Polka." Starting with a single softly played note, and building in crescendo into the famous "Roll out the barrel" chorus, the song has been played and cheered at hundreds of Boston College hockey victories.

But, on February 23, 1972—a cold and snowy night in Boston—the BC Band changed its usual victory song as the clock wound down on the Eagles' surprising 7-5 victory over archrival Boston University, the defending NCAA ice hockey champions.

That night, the band played "The Impossible Dream," because BC's revered coach, John A. "Snooks" Kelley, and his feisty team of mostly Boston-bred players, was improbably beating the top-ranked Terriers, 7-5, for victory No. 500 in Kelley's sparkling 36-year career at the Heights.

Coach John "Snooks" Kelley celebrates his 500th career victory—a 7-5 win over archrival Boston University—along with captain Vin Shanley (no helmet) and the BC team. (*Photo courtesy of Boston College Sports Media Relations*)

As the game ended, the cheers—and the music—rained down on Kelley and his players in recognition and appreciation of their remarkable achievement. A giant three-foot-by-five-foot cake, inscribed with "SNOOKS—500"—that had been kept in the BC Dining Services freezer in McElroy Commons in anticipation of the milestone victory—was hastily brought down to the rink and wheeled out onto the ice. BU coach Jack Kelley—a no-nonsense style mentor—embraced his BC counterpart at mid-ice and offered his congratulations, but was quietly steaming over the indignation of losing such a center-stage game to his longtime rival.

Needing but 13 more wins to become the first college coach to notch 500 career wins, Kelley had announced his retirement at the beginning of the 1971–72 season, offering BC administrators a full hockey cycle to choose a successor. The Eagles had seen All-America defenseman Tom Mellor leave school to join the US Olympic Team—the eventual silver medal winners in the Winter Games held in Sapporo that year—and BC was struggling along with a 12-14 record and had no hopes to qualify for the end-of-season ECAC playoffs.

Prior to the season, BC captain Vin Shanley, who lived almost across the street from the campus in Boston's Brighton neighborhood, had ordered round maroon and gold buttons stating "Year of Snooks' 500" that were eagerly snatched up by BC students and fans.

The previous weekend, the Eagles had surprised a heavily favored Clarkson team, 6-4, to begin a particularly challenging leg of the season's schedule that required the Bostonians to play four games in six days—three of them on the road. When BC beat Dartmouth in Hanover to celebrate President's Day on Monday, February 21, and capture win No. 499 for Snooks, the BC bakers readied the cake—but even the most optimistic Eagle fans figured that it would not be presented until the more-winnable Army game on Friday night the 25th, virtually ceding the Wednesday night contest against Boston University as an impossible task. BU had won 16 of the previous 17 games against BC, including a pair of meetings earlier in that season, and there was no doubt that beating the Terriers would be a high hurdle—even for a team motivated to win one for their soon-to-depart coach.

Boston College players set the stage for the big event by taking a carton of Shanley's buttons and using them to spell out a message on a white bedsheet that was hung in the McHugh lobby: TONIGHT'S THE NIGHT the improvised sign read.

"I still remember that night," Shanley, now an attorney in the Boston area, recalled. "They were one of the top teams in the country, but we had played a pretty good game against them in the Beanpot, even though we had lost 4-2. On the night of the game, throughout the entire BC locker room, we just had a feeling that something was going to happen. We all had the sense that this could be a great occasion to do this for Snooks against our archrivals. It magically just came together."

Shanley said that the normally bombastic Kelley did not mention the possibility of his 500th victory in his pregame remarks. "He didn't want to make it 'Hey, you guys need to go out there and win my 500th,'" Shanley said. "He didn't make it about him. He just gave the typical 'coach-speak.' It was me and some others—when Coach was out of the room—exhorting the rest of them that we had a chance to do something special that night."

BC's top goaltender, Neil Higgins, was not available for duty for the game, having injured knee ligaments in the previous week's win at Clarkson. Leading scorer Ed Kenty was forced to wear a plaster face guard after breaking his nose in Monday's game at Dartmouth. Several other BC players were nursing the flu.

The game was scheduled to start at 8 p.m., but in those days before the down-to-the-second structure of television time schedules, the coaches decided to play a "cat-and-mouse" game over which team would take the ice first. Finally, at 8:09, the Eagles emerged from their locker room under the east stands of McHugh Forum. A minute later the Terriers emerged from their quarters across the ice. The puck was finally dropped at 8:21.

Sophomore Ned Yetten got the call to play in goal just minutes before his team took the ice. "I was really scared out there," he would admit later. No wonder—BU's Ric Jordan scored on a blazing 50-foot slapshot just minutes into the game, and teammate Ron Anderson followed by tucking home a rebound to give the Terriers an early 2-0 lead.

BC never gave up, answering with back-to-back goals by Kenty (on a rebound of a Harvey Bennett slapper) and Jim King—one of the flu patients—who launched a curving wrist shot from the left corner that evaded BU netminder Dan Brady. BC had two goals on their first five shots, and the score was tied at 2-2 midway through the first period.

BU's Kelley decided to replace Brady, who had been bothered by a tender ankle, with recent Olympian Tim Regan. Regan fared no better.

The teams traded goals until BC took a 5-4 lead on another Kenty goal early in the third period, and the 4,300 who packed McHugh suddenly had a sense that an upset of magical proportions could be brewing. BU answered with a Bob Brown tally at 6:26 to knot the score again, but just 1:01 later, Kenty took a pass from Jim King and gave the Eagles a 6-5 lead they would not relinquish.

In the final minute, Regan skated to the BU bench in favor of a sixth attacker, and the Terriers tried to put the heat on young Yetten, who was playing his first varsity season. Suddenly, it was the rangy masked-man, Kenty, who fired BC's insurance goal into the empty net—his fifth point of the night—with just 12 seconds left on the clock.

The strains of "The Impossible Dream" filled the Forum air.

After the mandatory handshakes and coaches' hugs, a microphone was brought out to center ice and "Snooks" addressed the adoring crowd. "I doubt if I have ever been happier with this bunch of kids," he said to deafening cheers. "They demonstrated that if you have the will to win, you can overcome mountains—as they did tonight."

A postgame celebration was held on the basketball floor—of all places—of Roberts Center, a few yards up the hill from the "House that Snooks Built." Hundreds of fans attended and shared the victory cake and joined their cherished hockey coach in a rousing chorus of "For Boston." Outside, a brisk snowstorm continued to cover the ground.

The next day, University President W. Seavey Joyce, S.J., declared a rare school holiday; some thought that the closure was the result of the late snowstorm. Fr. Joyce would always maintain that the half-foot of snow that had fallen on campus overnight had nothing to do with his decision.

5

A NICKEL FOR A GOAL... A DIME FOR AN ASSIST

The Torch Is Passed to Len Ceglarski

Antony Ceglarski had emigrated from Poland to America, eventually bringing his wife and eight children to East Walpole, Massachusetts, where he worked long hours at the A. C. Bird & Son shingle mill to provide for his family.

After work most days, he would join his fellow workers at the local tavern to enjoy a beer or two; he would sit there and listen as his coworkers bragged about their sons' athletic skills. Antony, who never owned an automobile, had never even seen his youngest child, Leonard, play hockey for the Walpole High School team. In fact, he had never even seen a hockey game at all.

But he did understand the nature of team sports and what it took to win. Tiring of hearing all of the *braggadocio* about individual accomplishments, one night when he got home he made a unique offer to his athletic teenage son: "Lenny, for every goal you score, I will give you a nickel," the elder Ceglarski told his son. "But for every assist, I will give you a dime."

"That was the philosophy that I carried for all of the years that I coached," said Len Ceglarski, who became head coach of hockey at Boston

College in the spring of 1972. "Every year, I would tell the kids, 'If you don't pass the puck, you are going to sit on your rear end.'"

Ceglarski, a 1951 Boston College graduate, was captain of the hockey Eagles under coach John "Snooks" Kelley, earning All-America honors as a senior; was a valuable member of BC's 1949 NCAA championship team; won a silver medal as a member of the US Olympic hockey squad in the 1952 Winter Games in Oslo; and eventually became one of the most successful head coaches in the history of college hockey.

He was the perfect choice to succeed the legendary Kelley.

*   *   *

Len Ceglarski's path to Boston College was not an easy one. He had been a hockey and baseball star at Walpole High prior to his graduation in 1944, but like almost every young man of his generation, he accepted a diploma in one hand and a Selective Service draft notice in the other. When Ceglarski took the military entrance physical, doctors detected a minor abnormality in his bone structure, and since he had three older brothers already serving overseas, Len was issued a temporary deferment. However, his future remained unclear. He and his neighbor, Edward "Butch" Songin, the son of a Russian-Polish immigrant who worked alongside Ceglarski's father in the mill, had heard of the virtues of a Boston College education from the Rev. Leo Pollard, S.J., a teacher and hockey coach at Boston College High School who knew the Walpole families and tried to steer the talented prospects to Chestnut Hill.

But Len had taken the commercial course in high school and was clearly not ready to do college-level academic work. "I wasn't good enough to go to BC right away, so I went up to Huntington Prep, which at the time was located in the YMCA right next to Northeastern, and took some courses. My brothers and sisters took up a collection to send me there."

Ceglarski was now academically ready for Boston College, but during the war, the Eagles had been forced to downgrade their hockey program and had no scholarships to offer. "I didn't have any money to pay the tuition myself," he said. "I am proud to say that I worked two years in a paper mill—from 7 a.m. until 3 p.m. doing piece work every day, taking a half hour off, and then working the 3:30 to 10 p.m. shift driving a small truck for the company. I worked seven days a week. I was twenty years old when I finally got to BC." Rev. Maurice V. Dullea, S.J., the college's dour-faced faculty moderator of athletics, finally offered Ceglarski an athletic grant—but with the provision that he play at least two sports, hockey and baseball.

Boston College had little on-campus housing for students at that time, and Ceglarski did not have enough money to rent a room closer to the campus. "I was going to quit a number of times," he recalled. "We didn't have a family car. My brother Henry would leave the house at 6:30 every morning and give me a ride as far as Norwood where he worked. For the next four years, I hitchhiked from there up to BC, carrying my hockey or baseball gear as well as my schoolbooks. I don't think I missed more than three classes because I couldn't get a ride."

During hockey season, he would attend classes and do his studying during the day. He would then attend evening practices three times a week, most of which were held at the Boston Skating Club on Soldiers' Field Road from 9 to 10 p.m. After the team workout, he would load up his gear, hop on a bus to Central Square in Cambridge, transfer to the subway line that went to Forest Hills, and then board the last bus out to Walpole, getting home just about in time to start the whole process all over again.

Games were held on Friday nights in Boston Arena. When Len was a sophomore, Butch Songin's father—who owned an automobile—volunteered to bring Antony Ceglarski into the Arena where he saw his son play organized hockey for the first time. The gracious Songins also supplied both Ceglarskis with a ride back to Walpole after the long college hockey double-headers there that were the college hockey staple of the era.

*   *   *

Ceglarski had an illustrious playing career during an equally illustrious stretch of Boston College hockey. As a sophomore, he was a member of the Eagles' fabled 1949 NCAA championship team, and scored the tying goal in the third period as the Eagles rallied to win the title game over Dartmouth, 4-3; in his junior year, he led BC in assists (25—perhaps prompting $2.50 in rewards from his dad), serving as the principal setup man for top scorer Warren Lewis. As a senior, the left wing scored a team-high 21 goals and was elected captain of the 1950–51 squad. He finished his varsity career with 108 points—fourth-best in the Eagle record book of the time. BC won 47 games and lost only 14 during his playing career.

During a recent BC hockey season, Ceglarski was asked to return to campus to address Coach Jerry York's team that was preparing, once again, to play in an NCAA tournament.

"I told them, 'You know what? You guys think you are pretty good. But you know what else? We had eleven guys on our team in 1949 who could play as good as anybody in this locker room!' I was banging my fist on the table as I was saying this. They loved it!"

In fulfilling his two-sport "requirement" for a BC athletic scholarship, Ceglarski was the second baseman for the BC baseball squad. He teamed with fellow Walpole native Joe Morgan, BC's shortstop, to become the top double-play combination in New England. Ceglarski, a great natural athlete, led all collegiate hitters in New England with a dazzling .429 batting average in his senior season. But after graduation, it was Morgan, who also played hockey, who signed a professional baseball contract, advancing to play four seasons on major league rosters. He eventually became the popular field manager of the hometown Boston Red Sox for three and one-half years (1987–92).

* * *

After he graduated from Boston College in 1951, Ceglarski's Selective Service deferment expired and his draft number came up again. This time, he elected to join the United States Marine Corps and was sent to Officer Candidate School in Quantico, Virginia. There, he impressed the training cadre with his leadership skills, especially his ability to maneuver his platoon through the intricacies of close order drill—not an easy task with a group of new military recruits—and most certainly the mark of a competent teacher. One day, he was called from the rifle range and told to report to base headquarters "on the double." As he entered the administration building, he was surprised to see six other young Marines who had played college hockey for schools in Minnesota, Wisconsin, and Massachusetts also reporting as ordered. Boston Garden president Walter Brown had been charged with assembling a hockey team to compete in the 1952 Olympic Winter Games in Oslo, Norway, and he figured the best way to do it was to work with the US military to find qualified former college players who were already serving their country and could be quickly reassigned to the Olympic tryout squad.

When the US team arrived in Norway they found a bevy of European opponents who played a completely different style from the North American game. Ceglarski, always a

Former BC player Joe Morgan went on to manage the Boston Red Sox. (*Photo courtesy of Boston College Sports Media Relations*)

gentleman on skates as well as off, noted that "[t]he Swedes, the Czechs, and even the Germans would come down the ice and they would not go physically at you, but they might go at your ankles with their sticks. The guys who were the referees couldn't skate all that well and so those guys were getting away with just about anything they wanted." Even though Team USA coach John E. "Connie" Pleban, who had previously been a player-coach for the AAU Eveleth (Minnesota) Rangers, cautioned his players not to retaliate, the Americans got into scuffles with virtually every European team they faced.

Team USA was scheduled to play Poland on an outdoor rink midway through the tournament. The warm winter sunshine had melted part of the ice surface, and the teams were forced to wait several hours until the temperature dropped back below freezing to start the game. "We weren't supposed to mingle with them," recalled Ceglarski. "But if you got up to go to the restroom or something you would run into each other. That poor Polish team had the most terrible uniforms and equipment I had ever seen. Of course, I could speak Polish, so I was going to give them some sticks and other gear. Right away, they said 'No!'—figuring if they went back with American equipment they would get shipped off to Siberia or something. I was trying to tell them that my mother had been born in Krakow and both of my parents had come from the old country, but they did not want to hear any of it.

"Finally, the game started, and during the faceoffs, I was talking in Polish to this big guy—he must have been six-four," Ceglarski said. "He kept telling me that the Polish people were mad because they felt that the United States and the Allies had stopped the war too soon and let Russia take over Poland. A little bit later, I bumped into the guy and all of a sudden he wanted to kill me [laughter]. I looked around for the referee, but he was trying to call the game from behind the net and wasn't going to do a thing." Ceglarski got a rare five-minute major penalty for scrapping with the much bigger opponent.

Fortunately, the Americans beat the riled-up Poles that day, 5-3, and finished with a 6-1-1 record in tournament play, losing only to Sweden (4-2) and tying the eventual gold medal-winning Canada sextet, 3-3. The fine showing earned Ceglarski and his teammates a silver medal as the second place team in the final standings.

* * *

When he finished his hitch in the Marine Corps, Ceglarski accepted a non-paid hockey coaching job at Norwood High School and later was asked to consider a sixth-grade teaching post in Walpole where an unruly group of young students had forced two teachers to quit within a year. "The class had nineteen boys and three girls," Ceglarski said, but with his strict Marine Corps discipline and revered hockey reputation, he quickly got the wild group under control. The following year, he was hired as Walpole High's hockey and baseball coach, and in just his second year on the job, he directed the Hilltoppers to the Massachusetts State championship, where Cambridge Latin (coached by his old BC teammate Jim Fitzgerald) edged Ceglarski's team, 2-1.

The season was not quite over, as both teams were invited to the New England championships the following week. Walpole beat Connecticut entries Hamden High and Wilbur Cross High of New Haven, earning Walpole a chance to play Burrillville (Rhode Island) High in the aged, barnlike Rhode Island Auditorium for the regional crown. Ceglarski's charges tied the big game with just 10 seconds left in regulation, and then won it 2:10 into overtime to set off a wild celebration in the sleepy little Massachusetts town. More than 2,000 residents flocked to the town square to welcome the team home at 2 o'clock the next morning.

Two weeks later, another Walpole native, Bill Harrison, who had been coaching at Clarkson College of Technology for 10 years, decided to step down from his post. Bill's brother Cliff had also been a US hockey Olympian in 1952 and recommended Ceglarski for the job in Potsdam. Soon, Lenny and his wife, Ursula—whom he had met at the Boston Skating Club after a BC practice several years earlier—and their four sons (two more would be born later) were on their way to upstate New York.

*   *   *

Ceglarski coached at Clarkson for 14 seasons—from 1958 until 1972—and his teams won a staggering 71.7 percent of their games (254-97-11). His first year at the helm was a resounding success—winning his first college game against Providence by a 10-2 score (ironically in the same venerable old Rhode Island Auditorium where his Walpole High team had won the New England championship the previous winter). Clarkson also beat Boston College twice in Len's first season, trimming the Eagles by scores of 6-2 and 7-2.

In 1966, the Knights won the ECAC championship by beating Cornell, 6-2. Ceglarski's Clarkson teams never failed to qualify for the ECAC playoffs, and the Golden Knights advanced to the national championship tournament three different times.

In forging that successful college foundation, Ceglarski only had to look back to his dad's advice to shape his coaching philosophy.

"I hated it when somebody wouldn't pass the puck," he said. "In my first year at Clarkson, we were playing over at St. Lawrence and one of our kids came down the ice on a 2-on-1 and never even looked to the other man. Five minutes later, he came down the ice on a 3-on-1 and still wouldn't pass the puck," he recalled. "When he came off the ice I asked him if he saw or heard the other players on the break. He said, 'No, I didn't.' I said to him, 'You go to the end of the bench and when your eyesight and hearing get better you let me know.'

"I never had that problem again," he said.

"I made a rule at Clarkson that when somebody was coming up the boards with the puck, if one of our players got a penalty within three feet of the boards, he sat down for two shifts. The guy coming up the boards is not going to score a goal, so don't worry about him."

Ceglarski's tight-reined style of play became a Clarkson trademark. "We had the most disciplined kids I had ever coached," he said. "And every one of them graduated."

His coaching stint at Clarkson was largely a one-man effort. "I never had one assistant coach," said Ceglarski. "I was really overworked." In addition to his coaching duties, Ceglarski was responsible for the team's equipment, travel plans, and recruiting. Even wife Ursula helped out, mending and washing the team's game sweaters. "They once offered me a country club membership as an extra perk, but I told the athletic director that I wouldn't use it," he remembers. "I wanted to be able to spend the time I did have off with my family."

Ceglarski's pleas to hire coaching help fell on deaf ears, especially those of a Clarkson Athletics Board faculty member who vetoed every request that Ceglarski submitted to hire a full-time assistant coach. "But he [the faculty member] wound up going to Purdue, and I finally got approval to hire a coach to work with the freshman team," Ceglarski said.

"I don't know how [BC Athletics Director] Bill Flynn ever heard about that," Ceglarski said, "but out of the blue he called me one day and said, 'Would you consider hiring Jerry York for your freshman coach?' I didn't really even know Jerry very well at the time, but Bill told me I should hire him." Ceglarski continued to handle everything pertaining to the Clarkson varsity, while York coached the freshmen and, later, junior varsity teams.

The young protégé carefully watched the successful master, learning the fine art of coaching college-age athletes. He learned well. "Jerry wound up taking over for me when I went on to BC and had great success at Clarkson himself," Ceglarski added.

*   *   *

When "Snooks" Kelley announced that the 1971–72 season would be his last at Boston College, Flynn received applications from coaches all over the country. Ceglarski was not one of them.

"I never applied for the BC job," he said. "I got a call from Bill Flynn asking if I might be interested. I went down to BC twice to talk to him. After all of the years in Potsdam, I think all of us had enough of the snow. I said to Ursula, 'I would like to go back to Boston. How about you?'"

With the unanimous approval of BC's Graduate Board of Athletics, Leonard Stanley Ceglarski, at age forty-three, was announced as Boston College's head coach of hockey on March 24, 1972.

Ceglarski had filled his roster at Clarkson with a majority of Canadian players—talented young men who were grateful for the opportunity to attend the strong engineering school in the pleasant village of Potsdam in upstate New York and play Division I college hockey as well. Boston College, under Kelley's leadership, had never had a player from the Dominion.

"When I took over at BC, I had a meeting with Bill Flynn," explained Ceglarski. "It was our first meeting after I had taken the job. He said, 'What about taking Canadian kids?' I said to him, 'Bill, we could go to Montreal every year and I could bring down ten to fifteen candidates—and every one of them would be a good Catholic kid, a pretty good student whose parents wanted him to go to BC,'" he recalled. "But, in all my years at Clarkson, I had recruited only two players from Quebec. The rest were all from Ontario. I said that it would likely cost us. I didn't want to take kids that I hadn't seen before, and some of those Junior A coaches were bad news."

Flynn, he said, responded only with a couple of basic rules to which his newly hired coach was required to adhere: "He told me that he always wanted us to be competitive," Ceglarski said. "And, he told me never to go over my budget."

* * *

Coinciding with Ceglarski's return to the Heights in 1972 came a change in NCAA regulations regarding freshman eligibility. In response to the petitions of many schools that were facing spiraling costs in sponsoring freshman sports programs, the NCAA agreed to make students matriculating from high schools immediately eligible for collegiate varsity competition.

Mark Riley, who would go on to be a Boston College hockey cocaptain in 1974–75, was a member of the Eagles' last freshman team in the 1971–72 season. "Playing on a freshman team was a great way to launch your college career," said Riley, whose father, Jack Riley, was the longtime hockey coach at West Point. "We had a chance to get acclimated to the school and to college hockey. "

The natural chain of varsity transition was now broken, and Riley recalls that it had an immediate—and uncomfortable—result: "All of a sudden, those of us who figured that we were headed right onto the varsity had to say, 'Wait a minute—there are ten or fifteen new kids competing for those same spots.' It was like starting all over again.

"Lenny didn't know any of us. He had already started to bring in his own players. It created a lot more competition and a lot more uncertainty," Riley noted.

The transition did not show up immediately on the scoreboard, as Ceglarski's first BC team soared to a 22-7-1 final record, including a berth in the final four of the NCAA championship tournament held that year at Boston Garden. Included in the winning campaign was a 10-game winning streak that stretched from an 11-4 victory over Notre Dame on December 22 until an 8-7 overtime loss at New Hampshire on February 2. The long victory skein included wins over archrival Boston University (7-5) and national powerhouse Cornell (3-1) in back-to-back games in mid-January. It was BC's first victory over the Big Red in 13 tries since the rivalry with the Ivy League team was restored in 1965. As an added bonus, Ceglarski's new team won all 14 of their home games—much to the delight of the McHugh Forum fans.

A key to the rapid resurgence was the return of Tom Mellor, an All-America defenseman, who had taken a year's leave of absence from BC to play with the silver medal–winning Team USA at the Winter Olympics in Sapporo.

"He was like our own Bobby Orr, the way he could control a game," said Riley. "It was a huge addition." The Eagles also got spectacular play from goaltender Ned Yetten, who was voted the team's most improved player, and two of those freshmen newcomers, forwards Richie Smith and Mike Powers.

"I knew right from the start that we had some talent on this team," Ceglarski said as he prepared to the postseason. "What it amounted to was making a few changes and getting the kids to believe in themselves."

After bowing to Cornell, 3-2, in the teams' rematch in the ECAC final at Boston Garden, the Eagles moved on to the four-team NCAA championship tourney—also held at the venerable old Causeway Street barn.

"We had played in the Garden Christmas Tournament, the Beanpot, and the ECAC championship tournament in the same building," recalled Riley. "I almost think it would have been better if the Final Four had been somewhere else. The Garden was becoming 'old hat' to us, and I don't know if we were as fired up as we should have been."

The Eagles had their bubble burst in a big way, losing to Denver 10-4 in the NCAA semifinals. "There was a full house in the Garden," said Mellor, "and Ed Kenty scored a goal for us about 40 seconds into the game. I'm thinking to myself, *This is great*, but then Denver came back with eight straight goals, and that was the end of that."

In spite of the big loss to the Pioneers, Boston College applied a bit of salve to its wounded pride by beating Cornell, 3-1, in the consolation game on St. Patrick's Day. Defenseman Richie Hart took the third-place trophy and skated around the rink as if he were holding the Stanley Cup.

* * *

Ceglarski's amazing success in his first season at Boston College was rewarded with the Spencer Penrose Trophy as the national coach of the year—the second of three times he would capture the prized award (he also won it at Clarkson in 1965–66 and again at BC in 1984–85.) It was a great time to be a BC hockey player," added Riley. "Everything was new and exciting. Lenny put BC right back on the map."

That map didn't go too far. After having classes of compliant Canadian players at Clarkson who were happy to have the chance to attend a fine engineering school and play Division I hockey at the same time, Ceglarski was finding his BC roster filling with a lot of Boston-area superstars, some of whom spent more time reading their own press clippings than poring over schoolbooks.

There was also a crunch of players competing for roster spots since the new freshman eligibility bylaw was enacted. One scholarship player, Joe Marsh, was disappointed at his assignment to BC's new junior varsity team as a sophomore and did not want to wait for his chance to move back up to the varsity. He transferred to the University of New Hampshire, where he earned a varsity slot and eventually went on to become head hockey coach at St. Lawrence University.

The turmoil of departing players—either by choice or by decree—plus the usual attrition of injured players caused a pair of disappointing seasons: a 16-12 finish in 1973–74 when BC did not make the Eastern playoffs and a lackluster 11-15-2 record the following winter. "Kids were flunking out and not playing the way they could," noted captain Ray D'Arcy, "but Lenny was approaching it more like a father than a coach. He was more interested in doing the right thing rather than what it would take to win."

* * *

One of Ceglarski's strategies to ensure that none of BC's future problems would be of the self-inflicted variety was to expand the team's recruiting area. One of his most interesting recruiting tales took place in the middle of Manhattan, where he was scouting a young phenom who had learned the game on roller skates at a public school playground in the borough's tough "Hell's Kitchen" neighborhood. The player's name was Joe Mullen.

Ceglarski was tipped off to Mullen's potential by a couple of rival coaches: Lou Lamoriello of Providence and Army's Jack Riley. Lamoriello had briefly recruited Mullen's older brother, Tommy; Riley kept regular tabs on New York's Metropolitan League in his search for West Point hockey prospects.

"I basically learned hockey on roller skates," Mullen said. "We used to play in the asphalt schoolyard at the New York School of Printing right across from where we lived at 49th Street and 10th Avenue.

"The Metropolitan Junior League was initially started by Emile Francis, who was the general manager of the New York Rangers when they played at the old Madison Square Garden. The old Garden was right up the street from our house—you could look out our window and see it. My father worked on the 'bull gang' at the Garden for years.

"Anyway," Mullen continued, "back in the 1960s, Mr. Francis was taking a walk and he saw all these kids roller skating down the street with hockey sticks in their hands. He followed them to the schoolyard and started to watch us play. He said, 'I need to get these kids on ice.'"

The "New York West Siders" hockey club was established, playing its home games at the Sky Rink on 34th Street between 9th and 10th Avenues. Mullen's oldest brother Kenny was the first to make the team, and later younger brothers Tommy and Joe signed up to play.

Tommy was good enough to earn a scholarship to American International College, a Division II program in Springfield, Massachusetts. And several West Siders alumni eventually joined him there. "They were recruiting me," explained Joe, "and that would have been the easy place to go. But when I heard that BC might be interested in me, I decided to take a chance."

Ceglarski recalls the unusual recruiting effort well. "I took two trips down to New York to see Joe and the West Siders in action. The first time, I watched them play roller hockey for about fifteen minutes; then, we all got on this old, broken-down bus to go to an ice hockey game on the road. They had a big meal spread out in the back of the bus—lasagna, spaghetti, the works.

"They used to play in a rink that was smaller than regulation size, and when they could, they would practice at the Garden a couple times a week after the Rangers finished playing. The kids on the team were not particularly good skaters because they just didn't have the opportunity to practice. There's not a lot of ice in the middle of Manhattan!"

Ceglarski was impressed by Mullen's ability to put the puck in the net, regardless of the level of competition. "I went back to Bill Flynn and said I'm going to offer this kid."

Mullen recalls that he accepted Ceglarski's offer of a campus visit, enjoying the first airplane ride of his life as he took the air shuttle up to Boston. "BC was the only Division I school to recruit me," Mullen says today. "I was so nervous going up there. I thought that the school was beautiful. As they say, sometimes the school just finds you. There was just so much right about it."

When Mullen arrived on campus to start his freshman year, Ceglarski worked dutifully to improve his new player's skating skills that still showed the quick, choppy motions of roller skating.

"I'd bring him out on the ice with me and say, 'I'll follow you, and then you have to follow me' around the ice." Mullen adds, "My stride was off. Roller skating was more like running. In warm-ups, Lenny would have me skate behind Rob Riley. And try to imitate what he was doing." Riley, whose father was the longtime coach at West Point, had been well schooled in hockey fundamentals since he was a youngster and had a near-perfect skating stroke. "Finally, I started to get it a little bit," Mullen admitted.

Assistant coach Tom Hurley, who had been an All-America forward at Clarkson before joining the 1968 US Olympic Team, worked with Mullen to make him an even more dangerous scoring threat. "Early in my career, he grabbed me and said, 'You know, you don't always have to go top shelf with your shot,'" Mullen said. "'All you have to do is get the puck in the net. Go low sometimes, high sometimes, mix it up.'"

Mullen's newly found skating skills and scoring touch served him well: not only was he a member of four winning teams, but also the sharpshooting right wing set the all-time BC career scoring record with 110 goals in 110 career games, plus 102 assists for 212 points. He twice won All-America honors and was the leading scorer on the BC team that went to the finals of the NCAA championship tournament in 1978.

"I will always remember our first Beanpot [1976]," Mullen said, "which we won. I was lucky enough to play on a line with Richie Smith and Mark Albrecht in my freshman year. It was a lot of fun. Richie was such a great player—he could make things happen in a second. You had to be ready all the time, because he was such a great passer that half the time I didn't even know the puck was on my stick it was there so quick."

Later, Mullen went on to a starry National Hockey League career where he became the highest-scoring American-born player in league history, with 1,063 points (502 goals, 561 assists), and was a member of three Stanley Cup championship teams in Calgary (1989) and Pittsburgh (1991 and 1992). Joe Mullen is a member of the Hockey Hall of Fame.

"I really enjoyed my time at BC," he says today. "The people up there, my teammates, all the coaches were great. My stay at BC was an influence on my whole life. It has been tremendous."

* * *

Mullen's arrival at the Heights went hand-in-hand with Ceglarski's expanded recruiting effort, now bolstered by the addition of former Boston Technical High School and BC star defenseman Steve Cedorchuk, a recruiting specialist who knew Boston high school hockey like the back of his hand. In addition to Mullen, the Eagles signed fellow Met League player Paul Skidmore (Holtsville, Long Island); Chicago-born defenseman Joe Augustine; Minnesota schoolboy stars Steve Barger, George Amidon, Joe Caffrey, Paul Hammer, and Gary Sampson; and Mark Switaj and Tom Wright from Ohio. BC didn't forget the local players either, with South Boston's Billy O'Dwyer, Brookline's Mike Ewanouski, and Providence's Billy Army, among others, who gave the team a complete hockey and geographical mix.

The result was a string of very successful seasons: 25-7-1 in 1979–80; 20-8-3 in 1980–81; and 19-11 in 1981–82, but the Eagles always seemed to falter at playoff time, losing to Cornell, Providence, and Harvard in succession in the first rounds of the annual ECAC tournament.

* * *

The Eastern Collegiate Athletic Conference was the governing body of Eastern college hockey at that time. An umbrellalike organization, the ECAC provided administrative, tournament, scheduling, and statistical support to more than 200 schools engaged in dozens of team sports in all three levels of NCAA competition. Unlike smaller conferences or organizations, it could not focus entirely on a single sport or group of competing schools. In the early 1980s, the hockey-playing Ivy League schools proposed abandoning the ECAC structure for control of their own league play. Athletics directors from the major New England non-Ivy hockey-playing schools got together and formed the new Hockey East Association in July 1983. Charter members of the league were Boston College, Boston University, Northeastern, University of New Hampshire, and Providence College. A month later, the Board of Directors added University of Maine and University of Lowell (now UMass-Lowell), and league competition began in the 1984–85 season. (In later years, the Merrimack College, University of Massachusetts, University of Vermont, and Notre Dame were added; University of Connecticut was announced as the league's twelfth member in 2012.)

"It was [BC's] Bill Flynn and [Providence AD/hockey coach] Lou Lamoriello who really put the whole thing together," Ceglarski noted. "They never told anybody they were even in negotiations until everything was ready." Lamoriello agreed to become the first Hockey East commissioner.

Boston College won the first Hockey East regular season title—the first of 13 that the school would capture in the ensuing thirty years.

At the end of the 1984–85, season, the Eagles ran into the country's hottest goaltender, Chris Terreri of Providence College, as the Eagles and Friars met at the Providence Civic Center in the first Hockey East championship game. Terreri made a record 65 saves in holding top-seeded BC at bay until Providence scored a 3-2 victory in the second overtime frame.

The Eagles still qualified for the NCAA Tournament that year and faced the WCHA's Minnesota Gophers in a two-game total goals matchup in Chestnut Hill. Minnesota won the first game, 7-5, but the Eagles came roaring back in the decisive second contest to win the game by a 4-1 score and the total goals tally by a 9-8 count. From there, it was on to Detroit's Joe Louis Arena—home of the NHL's Red Wings—where Providence's Terreri again applied the brakes to the BC wagon, this time turning aside 62 Eagle shots in a 4-3 triple overtime heartbreaker.

*　　*　　*

One of the original aspects of Hockey East play was a partnership with the Western Collegiate Hockey Association in which members of each league would play home and road games against teams from the other. The interleague plan, which involved some fairly extensive travel arrangements, was enormously popular when some of the marquee teams were squaring off—Boston College, Boston University, Wisconsin, Minnesota, and North Dakota, for example—but the added costs and extended periods dedicated to travel were a burden to others. Teams from the opposing leagues did not always agree on style of play, either: Michigan Tech coach Jim Nahrgang once pulled his team off the ice against the Eagles when he thought the Hockey East officials were calling too many penalties on his club. UMD's Mike Sertich complained that his team was forced to play shorthanded for 15 of the first 30 minutes in another interleague contest at Boston College.

Ceglarski says that a victory during the 1985–86 campaign stands out as one of his favorites from the era. The Eagles had some ups and downs during the season, finishing fourth in the Beanpot, but eventually winning the Hockey East regular season race and subsequently earning a spot in the final four of the NCAA tourney at season's end.

During that year, BC played a two-game series at Minnesota-Duluth. It was hovering around zero when the Eagles arrived at the northern outpost, and the thermometer barely budged during BC's three-day stay. Adding more misery, the team had to walk from the hotel to the UMD arena for the two-game set and practice skates. The host Bulldogs pasted the Eagles 10-1 the first night, but Ceglarski had his team ready for the second encounter. "After that first game, their coach [Mike Sertich] must have shaken my hand ten times," Ceglarski lamented. "He had this big grip, and he would almost hurt your hand when he was shaking it."

In the second game, the Eagles turned the tables, nipping UMD, 4-3. One of UMD's goals came on a huge slapshot from the blueline by Brett Hull, son of NHL Hall of Famer Bobby Hull. Brett, who would go on to his own superb career in professional hockey, unloaded the big one-timer that was past BC goaltender Scott Gordon before he could even move his catching hand. "I never saw the puck," the startled Gordon told his teammates later. "I saw him wind up and shoot, but I never saw the puck."

This time, after the game, Sertich barely tapped Ceglarski's hand as the two met at mid-ice. "I said, 'Mike you've got to be kidding me,'" Ceglarski recalled. "Why don't you grab my hand like you did last night?" Sertich stared at Ceglarski: "Aw, you effin' guys from the East are always complaining about something," he said gruffly. Ceglarski laughed. "Every time I saw him after that, at coaches' conventions or what have you, I would keep my hand in my pocket."

Ceglarski was so ecstatic over his team's improvement in that game that when he finally reached the team locker room, he stood on a metal folding chair waving a large towel and leading the team in cheers. BC trainer Steve Bushee grabbed the back of the chair to steady it, as he feared the delighted Ceglarski was going to topple over.

* * *

The 1986–87 season was a difficult one, as the Eagles were forced to play every game on the road. McHugh Forum had been razed to make room for the sparkling new Conte Forum facility, and construction of the new Eagles' home had stretched into two years. All BC "home" games were played at Boston University's Walter Brown Rink or Northeastern's Matthews

Area—the new name of the old Boston Arena—that had been purchased and fully renovated by BC's Beanpot-brother school on Huntington Avenue.

Early morning practices at a variety of available rinks and extra hours spent on Brush Hill buses didn't faze the team, as the Eagles elevated to a 31-9 record— one of the best season showings in their history. The team won 26 of 32 Hockey East games and, for the third time, captured the regular season championship hardware. This time,

BC Coach Len Ceglarski celebrates the Eagles' 1987 Hockey East championship with his son Tim. (*Photo courtesy of Boston College Sports Media Relations*)

BC continued its surge into the HEA playoffs, stopping Maine 4-2 in the tournament finals to win the school's first Hockey East tournament crown. The winning goal for BC in the championship game was delivered by senior Tim Ceglarski—the youngest of Len and Ursula's six sons and the first to play for his dad at the college level.

The Hockey East title launched the Eagles into the first round of the NCAA playoff—a two-game, total-goals scheme against Minnesota that would be played at BU's Brown Arena. The Gophers took the first night's meeting by a 4-1 count, and even though the Eagles rallied in the second game, winning 3-2, the two-night goals total propelled the Minnesotans on to the Final Four.

*　*　*

Perhaps the best Boston College player *never* to play a home game at BC was defenseman Brian Leetch, who competed one year for the Eagles, having to play "home games" at Boston University, Northeastern, and Harvard while the on-campus Conte Forum ice rink was being constructed in 1986–87.

Leetch, from Cheshire, Connecticut, by way of Avon Old Farms School, followed his dad, Jack Leetch, an All-America forward for Coach John "Snooks" Kelley in the early 1960s, to the Heights. Brian made his own—and immediate—hockey impact at Boston College, breaking into the starting lineup at defense and having a record-setting rookie year: 9 goals and 38 assists for 47 points in just 37 games. He was the first BC freshman to capture first-team All-America honors and won the Walter Brown Award as the top American-born college player in New England.

How dominating a college player was Brian Leetch? BC Hall of Famer Ken Hodge Jr.—himself one of six players on that BC team who went on to play in the NHL—explained the BC breakout play that year: "We just gave it to Leetchie."

Drafted by the New York Rangers, Leetch could not refuse an attractive offer from the Broadway Blueshirts to turn pro, and he continued to showcase his considerable hockey talent on the world's biggest ice stage—the National Hockey League. He was the NHL Rookie of the Year in 1988–89; twice won the Norris Trophy as the league's top defenseman (1991–92 and 1996–97); was named to the NHL All-Star squad 11 times; served as captain of the Rangers for three seasons; and was a member of the Rangers' Stanley Cup championship team in 1994.

He also was a member of Team USA in three Winter Olympic Games (1988, 1998, 2002).

Brian Leetch was elected to the Hockey Hall of Fame in 2009.

* * *

In December 1988, the Eagles hosted one of the elite Russian teams, Moscow Dynamo, in an exhibition game in Conte Forum. The matchup almost caused an international incident.

Former Eagle Brian Leetch was inducted into the Hockey Hall of Fame in 2009. (*Photo courtesy of Boston College Sports Media Relations*)

On the afternoon of the game, BC Athletics Director Bill Flynn and head coach Len Ceglarski hosted the Russian team's head coach, the head of the Russian delegation, and various other visiting dignitaries ("I thought at least two of them were KGB agents," Ceglarski would say years later) at a luncheon in Jimmy's Harborside Restaurant, a well-known, traditional Boston dining room.

"You should have seen them," laughed Ceglarski. "Everybody ordered lobsters, and I don't know if they had ever eaten lobsters before. They started calling for glasses of vodka, and as the food arrived and they began eating, they slopped all over everything. They all had the melted butter running down their cheeks and were causing quite a commotion.

"Finally, Bill said, 'OK, that's it—no more vodka!'" The Russians were nonplussed.

That night, the hockey Eagles upended Dynamo, 6-5, as Tim Sweeney scored the winning goal in overtime, taking a perfect pass from McInnis for the deciding shot. The Eagles were actually undermanned in that game, as McInnis' original linemates, David Emma and Steve Heinze, were playing with the US National Junior Team at the time. It was a long flight back to Moscow for the Russian contingent, with several members reportedly still suffering from indigestion.

*   *   *

By the end of the 1980s, Ceglarski had named recruiting wizard Cedorchuk as his associate head coach and brought in UMass graduate Joe Mallen, a former goaltender, as his second bench assistant. Tim Ceglarski, Len's youngest son (of six), who had scored the winning goal in BC's Hockey East title game versus Maine, joined the staff as a graduate assistant. Ceglarski was ready to build a team for a run at the elusive National Championship.

They started with David Emma.

Emma, who had a spectacular schoolboy career at Bishop Hendrickson High School and played as a member of the US Junior Olympic team, was offered full hockey scholarships by a dozen Division I schools. He chose Boston College because of Len Ceglarski.

"He told me, 'You will have to earn a spot here,'" Emma said in recalling the hectic recruiting process. "A lot of the other coaches around the country told me that I was going to go on the first line right away and I was going to be on the power play and all of that. They promised me the world. Lenny didn't do that. He said, 'I believe in you and in what you can do at this level. But, you are going to have to prove yourself.'"

And prove himself he did. The five-foot-nine, 175-pound center from Cranston, Rhode Island, was placed on a line with Steve Heinze and Marty McInnis—all three of whom would play on the US Olympic Team as well as in the National Hockey League—and the "HEM" line became the top offensive unit in all of college hockey.

Few seasons in Boston College hockey annals were as exciting—and successful—as the 1989–90 season that brought the Eagles to within a whisker of the long-sought NCAA crown.

David Emma is BC's all-time leading scorer. (*Photo courtesy of Boston College Sports Media Relations*)

Once again, BC won the Hockey East regular season honors—not an easy chore with powerful opponents right up the street on Commonwealth Avenue and right up I-95 in Orono, Maine. "The thing that I remember most about my college career is how Boston College, Boston University, and Maine were all at the top of their games at the same time," Emma said.

In the Hockey East playoffs, BC and Merrimack split a pair of games, but winger Marty McInnis scored a tournament-record five goals to quickly decide the quarterfinal series in BC's favor, 8-5 in the rubber game.

An outbreak of measles among Boston's huge student population forced Hockey East administrators to cancel the championship rounds at Boston Garden, the usual site of the league's postseason fray. Instead, the games were played at the home rinks of the highest-seeded participating teams. This meant an automatic home ice advantage for BC.

BC faced New Hampshire in the semifinal round, and the underdog Wildcats held a 4-2 lead with only two minutes left in regulation. Emma scored on a power play with 1:46 left on the clock and defenseman Ted Crowley rammed home a slapshot from the point, with just 48 ticks left, to tie the game. Freshman Bill Guerin sent BC to the championship round when he scored at 2:21 of overtime.

That game was the final one ever coached by UNH's Bob Kullen, another of college hockey's true gentlemen. Bob had been a Division II All-America at Bowdoin and after graduating was picked to play on the 1972 United States team coached by John "Snooks" Kelley at the World Championships in Romania. Bob went into coaching and succeeded Charlie Holt at UNH in 1986. After his first year he contracted amyloidosis, an incurable blood disorder, and underwent a heart transplant. Former Boston College assistant football coach Dave O'Connor took over the team while Bob recuperated, then passed the reins back to him for two more years. Kullen fell ill again in the months after losing the playoff game at BC and died in November 1990.

Two nights later, BC won its second-ever Hockey East title with a 4-3 victory over Maine before 4,284 "measle-free" fans at Conte. Emma was the Eagles' big gun again, scoring the game's first goal in a short-handed situation just 35 seconds into the second period. Goaltender Scott LaGrand was named Tournament MVP by coming up with 34 saves in the HEA finale.

Twelve days later, BC hosted Minnesota in a best-of-three series, again at Conte Forum. After the teams split the first two games, Emma and his mates made sure the Eagles would punch their ticket to the Final Four. Just six seconds into the game, Emma cracked home a slapshot. When the dust had cleared, BC had a 4-0 lead, and with LaGrand turning in another masterful performance (39 saves), the Eagles had a 6-1 win and were heading to the NCAA title rounds. The PA announcer in Conte Forum that night was unable to contain himself with a minute to play in the third game when he announced, "One minute to play 'til Motown!"

The scintillating play of the consecutive series had excited the thousands of Boston College loyalists who packed the rink. After the game, Guerin grabbed a BC flag on a pole from a fan in the front row and skated around the rink. Sophomore Jason Rathbone held up a sign that read: BC-ING YOU IN DETROIT. The crowd roared its approval. The players raised their sticks to salute the fans—the crowd roared again. And again.

"I honestly thought that the roof was going to blow off the building that night," recalled Emma. There was so much energy and excitement. That was one of the greatest series I ever played in. I get chills just thinking about it."

Returning to the Joe Louis Arena in the Motor City, BC saw its championship dream end—in the most frustrating way.

First, underdog Colgate upset heavily favored Boston University to eliminate one of the true heavyweight contenders for the prize. All BC had to do was beat WCHA representative Wisconsin and they would have a realistic shot at the title. It was not to be: Wisconsin beat the Eagles 2-1 in a titanic defensive struggle.

"I think Wisconsin must have set a record for the number of shots blocked that night," said Emma, referring to the 19 pucks knocked down by Badger defensemen during the game. "I think we may have set a record for most posts hit too—it was that type of game."

Wisconsin scored a pair of power-play goals and acrobatic goalie Duane Derksen turned aside 27 BC shots—in addition to his defensemen's work—until BC's Mark Beran finally got BC to within striking range at 2-1. In the final minute of play, both Emma and McInnis had clear shots blocked by Derkson, who had only lost once in his previous 20 games. "To this day, I believe that that was the National Championship game," said Emma, who noted that Wisconsin waxed Colgate 6-1 in the next night's final game. "The energy, the willingness by players on both teams to sacrifice their bodies, was so apparent. Those are the games that are hard to accept. Even today, when I think about it, you know that you gave everything you had in that game—every minute, every second of that game—and when you come out on the losing end, it's not an easy thing to swallow."

* * *

The Eagles were tabbed to make a run for the title in the following year—and Ceglarski knew that he was nearing retirement and would have few chances left. "My senior year was the most disappointing of all my years at Boston College," reported Emma, who would captain the 1990–91 team on his way to becoming the most prolific scorer in Eagle hockey history (he had 112 goals and 127 assists—239 points in his 147 varsity games). "That BC team was the No. 1 team in the country pretty much the entire year, but towards the end, we had some off-ice issues that affected the team as we were approaching the playoffs. So, the team that I thought was destined to win the National Championships, the team that I think was built to win the National Championship, was out."

The 1990–91 team finished with another sterling record: 27-9 in the regular season and winning still another Hockey East season crown. But the wheels suddenly fell off the BC wagon at playoff time, as the club was unceremoniously bounced from the Hockey East tournament by Northeastern, 6-5, in the quarterfinal round. The Eagles then had to wait 16 days to start an NCAA quarterfinal series against low-seeded University of Alaska-Anchorage, and the Seawolves made the long trip to Boston and surprised the Eagles with two quick victories, 3-2 and 3-1.

The dream was over—and so was BC's run atop the Hockey East standings.

* * *

One bit of consolation from the team's disappointing finish was that Emma became BC's first player to win the coveted Hobey Baker Award as the top college hockey player in the country.

Emma had led the nation in scoring as a senior with 81 points, winning All-America and every other honor available to him. Officials from the Decathlon Athletic Club of Bloomington, Minnesota, had notified him that he had won the prestigious Baker Award and would be flown secretly to St. Paul to accept the honor at the conclusion of the NCAA Championship game that was being played there on March 30. When Emma arrived, he was brought to a small holding room in the bowels of the arena and told to wait for the end of the title game, when the trophy would be presented to him in front of the large media gathering expected at the postgame press conference.

Upstairs, Boston University and Northern Michigan were playing for the NCAA title . . . and playing . . . and playing. The teams played three overtime periods before the Wildcats beat BU, 8-7.

"I think it was about two in the morning when they finally announced the award," said Emma. "All the fans had gone home, and there were only about three or four media people left to attend the press conference. From that point on, they decided never again to announce the winner on the same night as the championship game.

"The Hobey Baker people had the best intentions in the world," added Emma, "but the game turned out to be a really long one, and there really wasn't anything that could have been changed. It was still a tremendous honor, and I am proud to be a recipient."

*   *   *

The next year—Ceglarski's last at the BC helm—was an Olympic year, and the Eagles' roster was decimated by a number of top players rightfully accepting invitations to compete for Team USA at the Winter Games in Albertville, France.

As part of Team USA's grueling training schedule, the pre-Olympic squad played a series of exhibition games against college and professional teams all across the country. BC's Emma along with Heinze, McInnis, Crowley, Guerin, and goaltender Scott Gordon were all on the USA roster, and BC's 1990 captain, Greg Brown, would later be invited to join Team USA in Albertville.

On October 10, 1991, Team USA arrived at Kelley Rink to meet the Eagles. After Boston Garden legend Rene Rancourt sang a rousing National Anthem, the sellout crowd noisily anticipated the introduction of players from both teams. Team USA players were introduced by name and their previous hockey organization. At the last minute, two-time Team USA Coach Dave Peterson, a hard-bitten former goaltender from Minnesota, decided to change his starting lineup.

"Starting at center for Team USA," intoned the PA announcer, "from Boston College. . . ." And the roar began.

All six slots in the Team USA starting lineup were filled with a former Eagle, and with each ensuing introduction the decibel level of the thundering cheers shot upward. By the time the announcer reached the name of the USA goalie, "from Boston College, Scott Gordon," the rafters of the three-year-old Conte Forum were shaking.

As expected, Team USA easily defeated the depleted Eagle team by a 10-1 score. The ex-BC contingent accounted for 11 points in the game, with defenseman Crowley and forward Heinze scoring two goals apiece and forward Guerin pegging four assists. One USA goal was a pure Boston College flashback, with Heinze scoring from McInnis (now a BC assistant coach) and Emma. In goal, Gordon only had to make 17 saves; Eagles' netminders Josh Singewald and Mike Sparrow were peppered with 65 shots.

In twenty-five years of Conte Forum history, there may not ever have been a game when a "visiting" team was as warmly welcomed and so proudly hailed by Boston College fans.

"That opportunity to come back and play in front of our fans was such a treat," Emma would say many years later. "The fans could not have been more wonderful. They were always great to me during my career, and it sure carried over to all of us that night. BC was instrumental in helping us all become Olympians, and it was tremendous to come back and share that special moment."

* * *

Back at BC, Ceglarski's team struggled in his final year, ending up with a 14-18-3 record. The team did send the veteran coach out on a pretty good note, however, beating archrival Boston University 3-2 in the team's final home game and then defeating the hated Terriers again 5-2 in a Hockey East quarterfinal contest down Commonwealth Avenue at the Brown Arena. A 7-3 loss to Maine in the Hockey East semis in Boston Garden on March 12 marked the grand gentleman's final game as a head coach.

"Oh, I just feel bad for the kids," Ceglarski told a reporter who callously asked how he felt about losing the final game of his career. "They haven't had too much success in this building over the years, I guess. But at least we were beaten by a team in our own league and the top team in the country. I'm proud of them."

Boston College is proud of its former captain and coach as well. In 34 years as a collegiate coach, his teams won 673 games (419 of those at Boston College), and he retired as the winningest coach in college hockey history. His teams played in eight "Frozen Fours" and four NCAA championship games and won six Hockey East regular season championships and two Hockey East tournament titles.

Len Ceglarski is a member of both the Boston College Varsity Club Hall of Fame and the US Hockey Hall of Fame. His hockey sweater was retired to the rafters of Conte Forum in 2004.

6

THE EAGLES' NESTS
Boston College's Home Rinks

In its earliest years, the Boston College hockey team practiced and played its games on outdoor rinks in and around Boston. Two of those rinks were built on BC's new campus in Chestnut Hill. Several other cities—Chicago, Pittsburgh, Washington DC, and Detroit—had built indoor, artificial ice rinks before the turn of the century. But Boston lagged behind, and all of the colleges had to play their games outdoors.

That finally changed in 1910, when the first Boston Arena opened on St. Botolph Street. The Arena played host to many events, including interscholastic and college hockey and games featuring traveling squads from Canada. The Arena ice was also available to rent for practices, and Boston College joined other local teams in practicing there when it could.

World War I brought cutbacks to many college programs, including BC's. The Eagles played two games in the Arena in 1918. In December 1918, the first Arena burned down. It was rebuilt on the same spot and opened just before New Year's Day, 1921. BC's first game in the new Boston Arena was on January 13, a 4-3 win over MIT. In 1924, the Boston Bruins entered the National Hockey League and made the Arena their home rink.

When the Bruins moved into the new Boston Garden in 1928, the Arena was home to college and high school teams, often scheduling college double-headers and high school triple-header tournament games along with a wide variety of sports, family shows, and even a rodeo that starred cowboy Gene Autry.

When the Skating Club of Boston opened in 1938, the Eagles scheduled practice sessions at the landmark Quonset Hut-style arena on Soldiers' Field Road in Boston's Allston neighborhood. By this time, Harvard had built its own on-campus ice facility, but other hockey-playing schools— Boston College, Boston University, Northeastern, Tufts, and MIT—built their practice and game schedules around ice availabilities at the two rinks. Scheduling of hockey time was challenging at the skating club—with BC often getting practice times at the end of general skating, sometimes as late as 9 or 10 p.m.

This all changed in 1958, when Boston College opened its own on-campus ice facility, McHugh Forum, an airplane hangar-shaped structure that was built to be an all-purpose facility in addition to its primary mission of providing a home for the hockey Eagles.

McHugh Forum was built on filled-in land on what used to be an MDC Reservoir—a twin to the current body of water that runs between St. Thomas More Drive on the eastern edge of the BC campus down to Cleveland Circle. The reservoir on the western side of More Drive that extended to the Newton line was declared as surplus by the state's Metropolitan District Commission in 1948, and BC purchased the property for $10,000 and gradually began to fill it in to expand the university's lower campus.

In early 1957, Boston College president Very Rev. Joseph Maxwell, S.J., announced a plan to construct three athletic facilities—a new football stadium; an ice rink; and a basketball arena on part of the filled-in land.

The stadium, called Alumni Stadium, in recognition of the Boston College graduates and friends who contributed the $350,000 needed to construct the 26,000-seat wooden facility, opened in September 1957. Roberts Center, the basketball facility, was financed by the generosity of Mr. and Mrs. Vincent Roberts, longtime benefactors of the school, and by a federal grant made available because the new building would house facilities—including a small indoor shooting range—for the Army Reserve Officer Training Corps unit that was hosted on campus at the time.

The ice rink was another matter. Fr. Maxwell thought that the new hockey facility should be a covered outdoor rink—much like the one that had been built on the Dartmouth campus decades before. Athletics Director Bill Flynn and hockey coach John "Snooks" Kelley pleaded with the Jesuit president to make it an enclosed facility so that it could be used year-round for a variety of university events. Fr. Maxwell finally agreed, and hockey alumni quickly set up a fundraising telethon in the university's old Development Office in the former Philomatheia Hall on Commonwealth Avenue to raise enough funds to underwrite the project.

They were successful in their efforts and raised enough money to cover a substantial part of the $800,000 construction cost. The new facility was named in memory of Rev. Patrick J. McHugh, S.J., a beloved Jesuit priest who had been BC's Dean of Studies in the College of Arts and Sciences from 1920 until his death in 1935. Born in Boston in 1885, Fr. McHugh had attended Boston College before entering the Society of Jesus. When he died, *Heights* editor Edward J. O'Brien '35 wrote of his passing: "He was man enough to convey his true spirit of cooperation to every student who attended Boston College in the past 15 years. . . . His earnest wishes for the success of Boston College men and the contacts he made in furthering those wishes made him almost the one permanent institution of Boston College. . . . His name was all but synonymous with that of the institution which he so conscientiously guided." Fr. McHugh was the first Jesuit who was not a saint or a past president of the university to have a campus building named in his honor.

But as eloquent as was Fr. McHugh's tribute, the building that carried his name was anything but elegant.

The ice surface in the new BC rink was 195 feet by 85 feet—the exact same as the dimensions in Boston Garden. There were more than ten miles of piping, laid underneath a green and white terrazzo floor, carrying ammonia-chilled brine to freeze the flooded playing surface. The rink crew would meticulously wax and shine the terrazzo each year in preparation for the many events that would take place when the hockey season ended.

The building itself was sparse—there was a front lobby, with a one-window concession stand, a portable wooden box office, and small public restrooms on either side of the arena entry doors. Lines of people attempting to reach all of the facilities would wind around the lobby during pregame warm-ups or intermission breaks.

Locker rooms were located underneath the stands on either side of the facility. Oftentimes, two games would be played in a single night—a freshman contest preceding the varsity faceoff—but there was only one shower area on each side, meaning that the visiting freshman team would have to use the main visitors' room shower—sometimes meaning a quick dash across a public walkway for players covered only in towels. On at least one occasion, the hot water tanks stopped working on game night, leaving visiting and Eagles players alike with a frosty—and quick—postgame wash.

During football season, visiting teams would use the McHugh Forum locker rooms and have to walk around the outside of the building—through spectator throngs—to get into Alumni Stadium. The BC football team dressed in Roberts Center, and players and coaches walked down the steep hill and through the front gate of the field on game day.

McHugh Forum seated 4,000 people, most of them along the sidelines—several hundred in each end zone. All seating was on long, board-type benches. There was not a seat back in the house. Two small press rows were dropped in the middle of the spectator sections—sometimes causing arguments if overenthusiastic fans happened to look over the shoulder of a sportswriter and didn't like what he was typing.

True to Fr. Maxwell's wishes, the building was truly a multiuse facility. Not only was it host to commencement activities, but was frequently engaged for college mixers and dances, concerts (Diana Ross and the Supremes and Chicago were among the prime attractions), and over the years an antique show, a circus performance complete with wild animals, the installation ceremony for the Episcopal Bishop of Massachusetts, and a trade show for New England funeral directors, with caskets and flower urns filling the space where power plays and faceoffs had ruled only weeks earlier.

* * *

McHugh Forum was formally dedicated on November 18, 1958, with a figure skating show featuring US women's champion Carol Heiss and 1956 Olympic men's champion Alan Hayes Jenkins. Eleven days later, the first hockey game was played in the rink, with Boston College beating Harvard, 3-1, on November 29. Future All-America player Billy Daley had the honor of scoring the first goal in the game just 23 seconds after the initial faceoff; Jim Logue, who would also go on to All-America status, notched the first victory in the McHugh nets.

For all of the thrilling hockey games played at McHugh Forum over the years, none matched the comeback victory that the Eagles scored against Providence College on February 27, 1960, when BC defeated the Friars 5-4 to earn a spot in the upcoming ECAC playoffs.

Trailing 4-3, with just 30 seconds left in the game, the Eagles controlled a faceoff in the Providence zone. BC defenseman Tom "Red" Martin passed the puck to forward Ron Walsh, who tipped it past goaltender Paul Gauthier to tie the score at 4-4-The clock never started—causing Providence coach Tim Ecclestone to climb over the dasher and run out on the ice in a fit of rage. The officials decided to allow the goal, but ordered 10 seconds to be taken off the clock.

With momentum on their side, the Eagles took the ensuing mid-ice faceoff and fired it into the Providence zone, where Owen Hughes tucked in a rebound to give the Eagles a 5-4 victory with four seconds remaining in regulation time.

Over the years, McHugh Forum was kind to the Eagles on the ice. The BC home-ice record was a sparkling 282-93-10, meaning that the Forum was just about the friendliest place on earth to be an Eagle. The only perfect season for BC in its longtime McHugh Forum home came in 1972–73—Coach Len Ceglarski's first year of coaching at his alma mater—when the team went 14-0-0. The next-best showing was the 11-1-1 mark by Coach "Snooks" Kelley's club in 1960–61. In 28 seasons, BC had a losing record in its home rink only once: a 4-7-0 showing in 1970–71.

Bob Sweeney scored the final Boston College goal in the old barn, closing out the scoring in a 7-1 romp over Maine on February 23, 1986.

Boston College's Pike's Peak Club—the hockey support organization—turned out the lights for the final time at McHugh Forum with a gala "Wrecking Ball" dinner on April 9, 1986. Fans attending the gala were presented with foot-long sections of the old bleacher seats with a small plaque commemorating the history of the great old hockey hall.

Sadly, the man who had made McHugh Forum such a trademark of Boston College hockey—Coach John A. "Snooks" Kelley—passed away the day after the final tribute.

* * *

In 1985, Boston College president Rev. J. Donald Monan, S.J., revealed plans to build a new, $25 million state-of-the-art hockey and basketball facility—one that would seat upward of 8,000 fans in modern comfort as well as house offices for BC's administrative staff and locker rooms and weight training and sports medicine areas for its expanded intercollegiate sports program, now numbering some thirty-one varsity teams. The building was planned on the site of McHugh Forum, so the BC hockey team had to find temporary game and practice facilities for the length of the project, which stretched out to two years as engineering and design changes prolonged the construction period.

A squash court in the Flynn Student Recreation Complex was hastily remodeled to serve as the locker room for the hockey Eagles while they waited for their new arena to be built.

"We had wanted to build a rink that was 200 feet by 100 feet—an Olympic-size rink," Ceglarski said. "It would have been the only one in the United States. Because there were big rocks on one end of the construction plot [the former stone banks of the original MDC Reservoir] we couldn't do it. We wound up with a 200 by 90 rink." Located physically in the City of Boston, Conte Forum would also extend to within inches of the Newton line, but did not cross the border—meaning that BC administrators would not have to obtain complex building permits from two municipalities.

For the next two years, the teams held practices at MDC Rinks in Cleveland Circle and Brighton—at BU's Walter Brown Arena and Northeastern's Matthews Arena, which was the same facility where they had practiced a half century earlier when it was the Boston Arena.

"Home" games were played at BU, Harvard, and Northeastern rinks.

"It was character building, I can tell you that," said David Emma, who came to BC while the construction was still underway. "Sometimes we practiced early in the morning, sometimes late in the afternoon. It was always changing." The team would commute to their workouts in a small fleet of vans, driven by coaches and managers.

"I remember when we would be practicing at the old MDC Rink in Brighton, and there would be leaves and other debris blowing in and getting all over the ice," Emma added. "The conditions were not perfect by any means, but we all knew coming in what it was going to be like, but it just made us appreciate Conte Forum more than ever. We really didn't know any better," he laughed. "We were just thrilled to be a part of Boston College hockey. Thrilled to be the team that was going to start the tremendous tradition that we all knew would be built inside Conte Forum."

The day of the first game finally arrived—November 1, 1988. The opponent was forever rival Boston University. In spite of heavy rains, more than 7,000 fans were on hand for the first contest in the gleaming new rink. The visiting Terriers proved to be an unaccommodating guest, however, spoiling the building's debut with a 6-3 win. The Terriers' Ville Kentala, a native of Finland, took the honor of scoring the first goal in the new building, firing home an unassisted 12-footer just 1:22 into the game.

BC's beautiful new sports facility, Conte Forum, was inaugurated on November 1, 1988, with a hockey game against longtime archrival Boston University. Boston College president J. Donald Monan, S.J., and BC Athletics Director William J. Flynn dropped the first puck in a mid-ice ceremony with BC captain Tim Sweeney (right) and BU captain Mike Kelfer. (*Photo courtesy of Boston College Sports Media Relations*)

*   *   *

The rink, built by the Richard White's Sons Construction Co. of Auburndale, Massachusetts, did contain one flaw that drew the ire of at least two opposing coaches, BU's Jack Parker and Maine's Shawn Walsh. Both had noticed that the team benches were not symmetrical to center ice—meaning that the visiting goalie would have to make an extra stride or two to reach his bench if pulled for strategic reasons in the final period. When they protested, it was allowed that the third period of games involving their two teams would be broken into two ten-minute segments, so that each team would have an absolutely equal placement. The benches were evened up during a construction upgrade to the building in 2006.

Conte Forum was named in honor of US Representative Silvio O. Conte, a longtime Congressman from Massachusetts, who played football while an undergraduate at Boston College. He had to leave the team because of a serious knee injury and eventually attended BC Law School, which launched him into his successful political career, eventually serving sixteen terms as the US Representative from Massachusetts' First Congressional District.

Throughout his time in Congress, Conte championed issues of higher education, health, employment, and human services.

On February 18, 1989, the building was formally dedicated, with Congressman Conte attending the event and delivering the keynote address. In addition to the official naming of the multiuse complex, the ice rink was dedicated to longtime hockey coach John "Snooks" Kelley, and the basketball practice gymnasium was named in honor of Frank Power, who had served as a freshman, assistant, and head coach of the sport at Boston College for 32 seasons, from 1952 until his death in 1985.

*   *   *

One of the more memorable "special" home games in Eagle hockey history took place on January 8, 2010, when the Boston College took on super-rival Boston University at an outdoor rink built at Fenway Park, the fabled home of the Boston Red Sox.

Kelley Rink at Conte Forum: the Home of the Eagles. (*Photo courtesy of Boston College Sports Media Relations*)

The rink was constructed for the NHL game between the Boston Bruins and Philadelphia Flyers on New Year's Day, but Hockey East commissioner Joe Bertagna recognized a good marketing opportunity when he saw one and persuaded BC officials to give up a December home game against the Terriers to move the game into the revered ballpark.

When the "Frozen Fenway" event was announced in September 2009, tickets were sold out in hours. More than 38,000 fans paid between $5 and $90 apiece to attend the college hockey spectacular in spite of the poor sightlines to the ice surface, which stretched from the first base line to beyond third base across the baseball diamond.

On game night, with the temperature hovering in the low twenties and snow flurries falling through the illumination from the park's giant light towers, the scene resembled a giant snow globe. When BC coach Jerry York and BU's Jack Parker met at mid-ice to do a brief television interview just before the puck was dropped, Parker remarked: "How lucky are we to be involved in this?" York answered: "Boston certainly has been good to us."

Each team wore special uniforms to commemorate the occasion. BC's sweaters had a green stripe along the bottom, matching the famed Fenway "Green Monster" left field wall; the Terriers had their usual "Boston" logo in the same script used on Red Sox uniforms.

The pregame ceremonies concluded with BC's honorary alumni captains, Hall of Famer Brian Leetch and fellow NHL stalwarts Craig Janney and Marty McInnis, while the school from the other end of Commonwealth Avenue was represented by Olympian Mike Eruzione, NHL star Tony Amonte, and the inspirational Travis Roy.

Then the real fun began. BU jumped out to a 3-0 lead, but the Eagles clawed back to within one, 3-2, in a wild third period. The game ended at that score as BC forwards furiously buzzed around the BU goal as the clock wound down, but were unable to send the game into overtime.

"This game was everything that it was made up to be," said BC defenseman Tommy Cross. "I know that it is something that I will remember for the rest of my life."

Boston College has played two other games at the "Olde Towne Field," beating Northeastern, 2-1, on January 14, 2012, and Notre Dame, 4-3, on January 4, 2014.

7

BOSTON'S POT OF BEANS
A Midwinter Staple

The Beanpot Tournament. What can one say about it?

The championship of college hockey in Boston.

The annual midwinter rite.

Not just an athletic must. A social must.

The start of trophy season.

That's all been said, many times. What else can one say about the Beanpot? That it is unique, and parochial, and a definition-in-action of Boston itself. So now let us begin.

Results of the games of the Beanpot Tournament used to figure in league standings. They no longer do. All games against Division I teams still affect college national ratings and rankings, so the Beanpot still "counts" in that sense. But in reality, the Beanpot sits in splendid isolation, an event unto itself in the (justifiably!) self-proclaimed "City of Champions."

Each February, the edifice on Causeway Street now known as TD Garden—in Boston's West End, remember, not the North End—becomes "under the highway," where the Jets and the Sharks met to have it out once and for all in *West Side Story*. Or else the Garden turns into the quidditch pitch, where Harry Potter's Hogwarts houses of Ravenclaw, Hufflepuff, Slytherin, and Griffindor renewed their endless pursuit of the golden snitch. Those matches of Jets versus Sharks or the evil Slytherin versus the noble Griffindor play out with a similar emotional backdrop

The Beanpot Trophy is college hockey's mid-winter prize. (*Photo courtesy of Boston College Sports Media Relations*)

to the Beanpot's—that of a medieval morality play.

The Beanpot is a yearly reunion of family and friends, an occasion to lift a glass and speak fondly of days gone by. It's also college hockey's annual Festivus ritual, when all the old grievances reemerge, and the unlucky puck bounces and the outrageous calls by referees get thrashed out yet again.

The Beanpot often is a coming-out party for new stars. It can serve as "our whole season" for playoff also-rans. It can be a setting for storybook underdog heroics, a comeuppance for haughty favorites, a bloody nose to the town bully, a rooftop shout of affirmed superiority, a launchpad for a flight to postseason glory, or the first step down the icy slope to perdition.

Over the sixty-two years of its existence, the Beanpot has been all of those things, at one time or another, for Boston College.

BEANPOT EST OMNIS DIVISA IN PARTES TRES

The first Beanpot era, from 1952 to 1965, saw Boston College take home the Beanpot Trophy eight times. Harvard was the winner four times, and Boston University was the champion once.

In the second era, the thirty-five years from 1966 to 2000, Boston University was the winner 22 times. Harvard was next with six, Northeastern had four, and Boston College three—one in each calendar decade.

The third age of Beanpot, since 2001 and still in progress through 2014, has witnessed eight Boston College championships and six for Boston University.

The Beanpot has been the focal point, for better but more often for worse, of Boston College's rivalry with Boston University. No matter that the Terriers were an equal-opportunity hegemon in their long era of Beanpot domination. They treated Harvard and Northeastern just as rudely as they did BC over those thirty-five years. But Beanpot time was almost always a special delight for BU fans and a maddening frustration for BC followers.

Six times in that second era, the Eagles finished first in Hockey East, and once they topped ECAC Division I. None of those very good teams took home a Beanpot.

The Eagles met the Terriers ten times in the Beanpot final during those years and defeated them just once, in 1976. That win was a huge upset by an eighth-place, rebuilding outfit over a powerful and confident first-place club. The round-one matchups were even most lopsided. BU took the opener 11 times and the Eagles beat them just once, in 1981.

Two wins and 20 losses against BU in the Beanpot, from 1966 to 2000. That's how bad the second Beanpot era was for Boston College. But on the other hand, the third age saw the Eagles win five Beanpots in a row, from 2010 to 2014. The best they'd previously done for consecutive wins was three, from 1963 to 1965.

MODEST BEGINNINGS UPTOWN:
IN KEEPING WITH A BOSTON TRADITION

The Beanpot Tournament is one of four singular phenomena that have shaped the long tradition of sports in Boston. The others are the Boston Marathon, the Red Sox and their lyric bandbox of a ballpark, and Celtic Pride stemming from basketball's incomparable dynasty of the mid twentieth century. All four of these unique members of the Boston sporting family were born in or near the city's Back Bay section.

The Red Sox first played baseball at the Huntington Avenue Grounds, where Northeastern University now stands. The inaugural 1897 Boston Marathon had its finish line at the Irvington Street Oval, not far from Copley Square. The Celtics and the Bruins played their first games in the Boston Arena on Saint Botolph Street, and later moving to the Boston Garden. So it was for the Beanpot Tournament.

The first Beanpot Tournament was just a four-team invitational that was designed to make a little money during a down time on the schedule, the Christmas holiday break. The four schools played and practiced there anyway, they figured, so why not get them all together, play for a prize, and sell a bunch of tickets?

Walter Brown, a hockey guy from way back and an energetic promoter, was in charge of managing both the Garden and the Arena in those days. It was he, according to Beanpot historian Jack Grinold, who determined that there would be a rotation of first-round pairings each year. Brown also thought that there should be a special trophy for the winners, something that would be symbolic. He sent assistant Tony Notagiacomo—a beloved fellow and longtime Bruins' timekeeper better known as Tony Nota—out to find a suitable memento. Tony came back with a silver bean pot.

The first games drew well, with a crowd of 5,105 showing up on December 26, 1952. BU beat Northeastern 4-1, and Harvard slipped by Boston College 3-2 in overtime. The Eagles' first Beanpot goal was scored by Frank O'Grady on a rink-length rush in the first period. That tied the score at 1-1. The Eagles took a brief 2-1 lead on Billy Maguire's goal off Sherm Saltmarsh's centering pass.

BC could not hold on, however, and the game went to overtime. Harvard's Walt Greeley scored the game winner on a power play at 3:51. BC's Jack Canniff had tumbled into goalie Joe Carroll and partially impeded his efforts to stymie Greeley. Carroll was in goal the following evening and recorded the Beanpot's first shutout, a 2-0 win over Northeastern.

The Beanpot moved to the Garden in January 1954. The Eagles gained a measure of revenge by knocking off Harvard 4-1 in the final. It was a tight game, with Jimmy Duffy and Bob Gallagher giving the Eagles a 2-1 lead that they nursed into the final period. Bob Babine scored on a break-away to clinch things at 16:15 of the third period.

Babine was chosen tournament MVP, even though Duffy had tallied a pair of goals in the championship game and amassed a total of five points in the two games. In the first round, the Eagles topped Northeastern 8-5 before a Garden crowd of only 711 hardy souls. Attendance would build slowly over the first decade, not hitting the ten-thousand mark until 1960 and finally selling out the Garden for the first time the following year.

RED MARTIN, THE 60-MINUTE MAN

One old and familiar bit of Beanpot lore is defenseman Tom "Red" Martin's playing the entire game of the 1961 championship final and taking home the Most Valuable Player Award. True, but with an asterisk. Martin had a minor penalty in the game; he skated for 58 minutes, not 60.

Tom was a three-sport athlete who always kept himself in fine shape. He also played first base for the Eagles' baseball team that made it to the College World Series in 1960 and 1961. He routinely played 50 minutes per hockey game anyway. It was more difficult in the packed and hot Boston Garden than in chilly little college rinks, but hardly a superhuman feat for Red Martin.

Tom is prouder of scoring the winning goal than he was of playing at much as he did that evening.

"Billy Hogan drew back a faceoff to me. I was a right-handed shot. A kid from Harvard came out to block it, and my shot caught the left inside post," said Tom.

That was BC's third goal, scored at 10:06 of the third period. The Crimson got one back to narrow the margin to a single goal again. Martin's classmate Billy Daley scored on a wraparound to clinch the win with 2:29 to play. Hogan had opened the scoring in the first period and assisted on Jack Leetch's second period goal. Jim Logue made 30 saves in the BC net to just 17 for Harvard goalie Bob Bland.

It was the first time that attendance in the old Boston Garden hit the magic number of 13,909, a capacity crowd and the largest to witness a college game there since 1931.

Snooks Kelley waxed particularly eloquent after the game. He said afterwards, "I've said I thought we were the best team in New England, even when we lost a couple. But now I know we are the best in the East. Of that I feel positive. That Jimmy Logue is the best goalie in the business. Look what he did tonight. Red Martin is as good a defenseman as anybody will ever find. Billy Daley is terrific. Those sophomores—Billy Hogan, Ed Sullivan, Jack Callahan, Jack Leetch, Ken Giles, and the rest. Tonight they were wonderful. They wouldn't be denied.

"You can stop a Daley two times. He'll get in the third time. You knew Red Martin would come through. Men like these can't be stopped forever. And they weren't."

Snooks might have gotten a little carried away in his euphoria. Harvard had beaten the Eagles twice already and was missing three of its regulars in the Beanpot. They didn't lose another game and finished 18-4-2 to BC's 19-5-1. Tom Martin, looking back on it all, says simply, "It was a great rivalry."

Few people of that era appreciated the BC-Harvard rivalry as did Tom Martin. He grew up in North Cambridge and spent many hours skating and scrimmaging one-on-one with a student named Bill Cleary on the near-perfect ice surface at the Crimson's Watson Rink. He played high school hockey at Cambridge Latin under Jimmy Fitzgerald, scorer of the winning goal in BC's 1949 NCAA championship game against Dartmouth.

Martin initially decided to play his college hockey for Cooney Weiland at Harvard. He informed Fitzgerald, who asked him to go and let Mr. Kelley know. That Mr. Kelley was Snooks, who taught social studies in the school. Young Martin dutifully went to see Mr. Kelley, who promptly summoned a substitute to monitor his class. He brought Martin to the teacher's lounge and laid the full Catholic trip on the lad, finishing his pitch with, "And your mother would want you to go to Boston College."

Whether Tom's mother Anne ever had expressed a preference for Tom's postsecondary schooling, we don't know. But the Catholic angle hit home with Tom. Anne, widowed when Tom was two, lived in a house owned by Saint Peter's Parish. Tom sold newspapers at Sunday masses from the time he was in the third grade until after college. So even though he lived about a mile from Harvard and learned his hockey there, he was going to BC.

Martin and Daley made the floater play a staple of the BC attack. They liked to pull it late in the game, to "send 'em home happy," as the wisecracking center Daley would say in calling for the floater. Daley would win a defensive zone draw back to Martin. Tom would retreat behind the net and watch as the opposing defensemen moved laterally out on the blue line. Daley would then sprint up the ice, his diagonal path taking him through the gap between the defensemen. Martin, emerging from the other side of the cage, would hit the streaking Daley with a long pass and send him in alone for the score.

The floater play worked many times, with Billy Daley getting the goal and Tom Martin the assist. But in the 1961 Beanpot, it was Tom Martin who scored the crucial goal. He never came off the ice, save for the two minutes of his penalty, and the 13,909 who were there that evening saw a feat of endurance that has never since been duplicated, and almost certainly never will.

The first time Boston College and Boston University met in a Beanpot final was on February 5, 1957. The game went to overtime before "the season's best record crowd for college hockey, 4,052 paid," as the *Globe's* Leonard Fowle wrote. He also described Joe Celata's winning goal as coming from an "impossible" angle. BC had trailed the whole game before finally tying the score, but went behind 4-3 with 1:34 to play. Ned Bunyon's second goal of the game tied it back up for BC at 19:07.

In 1963, both games of the first round went into overtime. Boston College nipped BU 2-1 when Billy Hogan backhanded home Jack Leetch's rebound. The following week the Garden's third sellout crowd showed up to watch the Eagles take their first of three consecutive Beanpots with a 3-1 win over Harvard.

The Eagles-Harvard final in 1963 would be the last time until 1981 that the two teams played for the Beanpot championship. It was a "torrid and rugged" encounter, according to Fowle. Gene Kinasewich got Harvard's only goal of the game in the first period to give the Crimson the lead, tipping a shot from the point past goalie Tom Apprille.

The Eagles got that one back late in the second period when Pete Flaherty scored with a shot from the right boards. But the play that's most often recalled from that period was the one that culminated the game-long jousting and jockeying between Kinasewich and Leetch. The teams were playing four a side when Leetch "floored Kinasewich after receiving what looked like an elbow check."

Both of BC's third period goals were scored on power plays and were set up by Hogan. He passed from behind the net to captain Paul Aiken for the winning score. Leetch's game winner came with 4:28 to play. Harvard only managed 16 shots on goal to 36 by BC.

Boston University was already involved in a serious rebuilding program under coach Jack Kelley, then in his second year. The Terriers held a 4-2 lead after two periods, but the Eagles' John Cunniff scored twice in a four-goal third-period rally to take the Beanpot 5-4. Cunniff earned the first of his two Beanpot MVP awards.

The following year, 1965, BC again faced the Terriers in the final. To get there, however, they had to get by Harvard in overtime on a goal by a sophomore named Jerry York. The youngster, who also had the game's first penalty for an illegal check, took a pass from Fred Kinsman and beat goalie Bill Fitzsmmons at 2:41 of the overtime. Jim Mullen, Phil Dyer, John Moylan, and Pete Flaherty had the other Eagle goals.

Cunniff took center stage again in the final, scoring twice and assisting on a third goal in a 5-4 win over the Terriers. Goalie Pat Murphy, who had been cut from the squad the previous year, had 42 saves. Nineteen of them came in the first period when he twice stopped BU's Ken Ross on breakaways. But Cunniff was the driving force once again. The *Globe's* eloquent columnist Bud Collins called him "The Madman of Beanpot" who was "the most valuable inmate of a mental ward called the Beanpot Hockey Tournament."

John Cunniff, winner of the 1964 Beanpot Tournament MVP Award, accepts the honor from the 1963 recipient, Bill Hogan III. (*Photo courtesy of Boston College Sports Media Relations*)

Collins continued, "The worst thing that happened to Boston University was Cunniff. . . . The Eagles knew they were going to win when he scored his first to shove them ahead 3 to 2. They had been behind 2 to 0. This goal was a masterpiece that shook the Terriers soon after they had benefitted from a penalty. . . . Fran Kearns pushed him a pass at the blue line. Cunniff was gone and it was just he and John Ferreira, the B.U. doorman, playing the game as nine others watched.

"With a magnificent fake he pulled Ferreira from the net—as though he had a vacuum cleaner instead of a stick—and inserted the puck into the right corner. Cunniff was born with a silver spoon in his mouth that turned out to be a hockey stick. . . . He was also born, apparently, to preside over the Beanpot madness while at B.C. . . . The Bean Pot syndrome affects increasing numbers in our town every year. You can't get a ticket unless you scream like an elephant who's forgotten his mate's birthday. Our enemies think Americans are soft, but if we could send the appreciators of B.C. hockey to Viet Nam, they'd chase Ho Chi Minh back up his trail."

That 1965 win turned out to be the final game in the first era of Beanpot history. Cunniff was a senior the following year, 1966, and he scored one of BC's goals in the 6-4 opening round loss to BU. He, Dick Fuller, and York all scored to give the Eagles a 3-0 lead by midway through the game. The Terriers tied the score at 3-3 by the second intermission, however, and got three more in the third. Bruce Fennie and Fred Bassi each scored twice for the Terriers, the new kings of Beanpot who were just launching a long reign.

The architect of that reign was Kelley of BU, a stern taskmaster and superb tactician who quickly became the bête noire of Boston College fans. He recruited both in Canada and in America, and he quickly built a pipeline of superior talent. He stayed at BU only ten years, but his success permanently changed the landscape of Eastern college hockey and of the Beanpot. His teams always were at their best when Beanpot time rolled around, and his successor Jack Parker was able to continue the Terriers' winning tradition.

Kelley explained his approach to challenging Boston College, unseating the Eagles from their Beanpot perch and establishing his own dynasty down the street.

"When I first got to BU, talent was lean. We had to get serious in our recruiting to get up to the level of BC and Harvard at that time. BC was a real powerhouse, and I knew all about them because I'd coached against them at Colby. So I was well steeped in the traditions of Boston College hockey.

"You can't live inside 128 and not know what the Beanpot is all about, and know how important it is to anyone who supports the colleges. So sure, we put a lot of emphasis on it.

"I had such great respect for Snooks and I loved coaching against him. He, Cooney Weiland, Eddie Jeremiah, and Herb Gallagher did so much for hockey way back then, getting it recognized and bringing it to the fore-front. What they've done is probably forgotten today. Snooks in particular. I enjoyed playing against his teams."

Though his BU teams were a particular nemesis for BC, Kelley respected the athletes who played for Snooks. Later on, he pursued many of them to play for his first professional team, the New England Whalers. Those he signed included Cunniff, Tim Sheehy, Kevin Ahearn, Tom Mellor, and Paul Hurley.

Cunniff was the oldest of the group, and Kelley's assessment of him was that "[h]e could float the whole game and then just explode. You think you had him contained, he'd be playing along with it, then an opportunity would come up, and he'd go and put the puck away on you."

But in 1966 the Cunniff era drew to a close, and the long dry spell for Boston College in the Beanpot had begun. It would be almost a half century—until 2010 and 2011—until the Eagles would win back-to-back Beanpot championships again.

THE MOST VALUABLE PLAYER EVER—WHO WASN'T

Records are made to be broken. Some day, a goaltender will make more saves in a Beanpot game than Jim Barton made in 1970. But for the next forty-four years and counting, nobody could surpass the incredible single-game performance by the junior from Needham, Massachusetts. Jim stopped—somehow, with knee, glove, stick, and skate—52 shots by the swarming, blood-lusting Boston University Terriers in that year's championship round.

Barton's heroics were not enough. The Terriers prevailed 5-4, riding Wayne Gowing's third-period hat trick to yet another victory over the

Eagles. Gowing was one of those interchangeable parts that BU coach Kelley had taken and molded into a fighting machine.

Fate and karma were all on the side of Boston University in those years, but Jim Barton almost sent the fates down to defeat. Almost. Gowing was seated on his duff in front of the net when he scored the winning goal with 2:54 to play. The press-box denizens gave the MVP Award to Mike Hyndman, a superb player and always a menace to the Eagles. But Hyndman was the wrong choice. Any BU player would have been the wrong choice. No one has ever been more valuable to his Beanpot team than Jim Barton.

By the time the 1970 Beanpot final rolled around, BU under Jack Kelley had gained near-total domination of the rivalry with Boston College. They'd won ten of the last 11 meetings, most of them by comfortable margins. That season, BC had started off well but was past its peak and set to take a fall. BU was young, brash, and aggressive, the rough draft of the near-invincible NCAA champion teams of 1971 and 1972.

When it was all over, BU's Kelley came over to Barton and said, "You became a big-time goaltender tonight." Jim had almost gone to play for BU and had been offered a partial scholarship.

Barton had backstopped Needham High to the state title in his senior year, and he also attended Kelley's hockey camp as a youth. Barton was an outstanding athlete, captaining the track team and quarterbacking the football team. He had to prep a year to get ready academically, and money became a big part of his decision. BC offered him a full scholarship. Jim felt so bad about turning down Jack Kelley that he asked his father to make the phone call to BU to inform the coach.

The only year in which Barton played as a BC regular was 1969–70, his junior season. He'd waited for George McPhee to graduate the previous year. The following season, BC coach Snooks Kelley gave the starting job to sophomore Neil Higgins.

Barton shut out Northeastern with 21 saves in the Beanpot's first round. For the finale, BC lost its fine right winger Paul Schilling to a suspension for fighting. Schilling always performed well against BU. In fact, another of his fights led to the only win by BC over BU between 1965 and 1973. In February 1969, in a game at Boston Arena, Schilling squared off against BU's bruising captain, defenseman Billy Hinch. Schilling clearly got the better of it. He toppled Hinch to the ice and stood above him, whaling the BU leader about the face with a flurry of lefts and rights that would have drawn admiring comments from old-time NHL pugilists like Leapin' Lou Fontinato and Terrible Ted Lindsay. For once in the series, BU lost its mojo and the Eagles romped over their rivals 7-3.

On the Friday between 1970 Beanpot rounds, a thuggish band masquerading as hockey players and wearing RPI uniforms came to BC and took a 13-6 pasting. As the *Globe*'s Bob Monahan put it, RPI was "a team that seemed to carry hatchets instead of sticks." Schilling, never one to back down from a battle, responded to a hacker by the name of John Renwick, took him on, and got tossed by referees Jack Garrity and Joe Quinn. He had to sit out the next game, the Beanpot final.

Boston College dropped RPI from its schedule for six years after that debacle. And it wasn't the first time that BC terminated its play against the boys from Troy. The series stopped for three years in the early 1960s after RPI fans in the stands threw rosary beads at the Eagles as they skated off the ice.

Three nights later, Coach Snooks Kelley tried to compensate for the loss of Schilling by double-shifting his best player, Tim Sheehy, at center on one line and right wing on another. It didn't work. Still, by the end of two periods, Barton had made 33 saves and the Eagles were somehow clinging to a 3-1 lead. But when the third period rolled around, as the *Globe*'s columnist Ray Fitzgerald put it, "Reality reared its ugly head."

"It was a shooting gallery. A target practice," said Barton. "I didn't have time to breathe. But the biggest thing I remember [is] just the onslaught. On the winning goal the puck came across and hit a skate. I charged out of the net and went to Bobby Barry the referee, who was from my hometown. I tried to tell him it went in off the skate, but he told me 'No, Jimmy, it's good.'

"You couldn't play on a better stage. The crowd noise was deafening. For 60 minutes. Incredible. They say you can't hear the crowd when you're playing. That's bull."

The Beanpot loss was crushing, if predictable. It was the true beginning of the end for that season's team and for winning hockey at the Heights until Len Ceglarski arrived. The Eagles lost five of their last seven games and made an early playoff exit.

None of that was the fault of Jim Barton, the best single-game goaltender and Most Valuable Player who never received the accolades he deserved

MOST GOALS IN A GAME: MIKE POWERS

Some day, a goalie will make more saves in a Beanpot game than Jimmy Barton. Some day, a forward will score more goals in a Beanpot game than Mike Powers. Mike was a freshman in 1972–73, and he scored five times, including the game winner in overtime, when Boston College defeated Northeastern 9-8 in the first round of the Beanpot.

Harvard immortal Bill Cleary had five goals in a 12-3 romp over Northeastern in 1955. Boston College's Eddie Sullivan had five in a 15-1 cakewalk over the Huskies too. But in 1973, what should have been another easy win turned into a Keystone Kops episode, a nail-biting escape, and a little-deserved ticket to the final.

Coach Ceglarski was livid after the game, telling reporters that "we were so undisciplined that it made me sick." He had a point. The Eagles had gone to sleep and blown two comfortable leads, much to the delight of the late-arriving crowd that sensed a giant upset and cheered lustily for the perennial doormats, the Huskies.

Powers was on a line with Richie Smith and Bobby Reardon. Ceglarski had put the trio together around Christmas time after a choppy start to the season. In the Beanpot opener, they accounted for a total of 13 points.

Powers had his first four goals in the early going when BC surged out to a 5-1 lead. Northeastern chipped away to make it 5-3, and BC goalie Ned Yetten came through with a couple of spectacular saves to stave off further disaster midway through the second period. The teams traded goals, making it a 6-4 BC advantage after two.

When Northeastern clawed to within a goal early in the third period, BC's Chuck Lambert and Jim Doyle responded to widen the gap to 8-5 with 11 minutes left. That should have been ample cushion. It was anything but that. Charlie Huck, Terry Toal, and Huck again, this time with 1:56 to play, tied the score at 8-8. The crowd was roaring for BC blood.

The Eagles regrouped and somehow got their offense going in the overtime. NU goalie Todd Blanchard stoned Powers twice before the Malden freshman ended it all at 6:56. He and Richie Smith fashioned a 2-on-1—Smith penetrated deep and dropped the puck back to Powers, who poked it past Blanchard.

For Mike, that game is by far the fondest memory of a two-year BC career. He had been set to go to Boston University after preparing at New Prep. But once BU passed over recruiter Bob Crocker as its successor to Jack Kelley, Powers made a visit to BC and received a scholarship offer from Ceglarski.

"It was the kind of game when I could have got six or seven goals," he said. "I scored one on a slap shot. On another one I was down on my knees in front of the net, the puck came to me, and I just chipped it over the goalie.

"On the winner it was a 3-on-2. Nowadays they don't even have 3-on-2s because everybody skates a hundred miles an hour. But I remember giving it to Smitty, he gave it back to me, I gave it back to him, and then when the defenseman moved toward him, I broke for the net, he gave me the puck, and I put it in."

Mike Powers scored the only goal of the 1973 final game against BU when the Eagles lost 4-1. The following year, when BC lost twice and finished fourth in the Beanpot, he had one goal and two assists. In two seasons and four games, Powers collected nine points. That total makes him the Beanpot's seventh all-time leading scorer on a points-per-game basis with 2.25. Harvard's Joe Cavanagh is the tournament's all-time scoring leader. He played six games over three years and tallied 19 points, a 3.17- points-per-game mark. Next on the all-time list are BC's Tim Sheehy and BU's Bob Marquis. They each played six games and had 16 points for a 2.66 PPG record. Others just ahead of Powers, all with 2.33 PPG, are BU's Shawn McEachern, Northeastern's Art Chisholm, and BU's Vic Stanfield.

After 1973–74, Powers turned pro and attended training camp for Jack Kelley's New England Whalers. He ended up playing five years in the International League. In his first IHL campaign, he teamed up with BC's

Ed Kenty on the Columbus Owls and racked up 100 points in seventy-six games. Not bad at all, but nothing like those five goals on the first Monday of February 1973.

TWO SHORTHANDED GOALS ON THE SAME PENALTY

It had been over a decade, eleven Beanpot disappointments and counting, when the 9-9-1 Eagles took to the ice against Northeastern for the first round on February 2, 1976. Oh, there had been a few hopeful signs, like beating Cornell in Ithaca, tying Harvard, and a close 4-2 loss to Boston University. The Terriers entered the Beanpot with a 14-2 record and were again the overwhelming favorite.

Three freshmen—Joe Mullen at wing, Joe Augustine on defense, and Paul Skidmore in goal—had kindled a good deal of hope in the Eagles' prospects for the coming years. But 1976 looked like another year of biding time on the Beanpot watch—and expectations were even lower because the Eagles had finished fourth in the tournament for each of the previous two years.

BC barely got by Fernie Flaman's Huskies, who hadn't been to the finals since 1967. The Eagles twice took two-goal leads and NU twice rallied to within one. Several times, particularly in the second period, Huskies on the attack had excellent scoring chances but misfired. NU drew to within a goal with 3:33 left. They had three offensive-zone faceoffs in the last minute after pulling the goalie.

Augustine's empty-net goal, his second of the game, with four seconds left gave the Eagles their escape. Paul Barrett also scored twice, Mullen had one goal, and Skidmore made 27 saves to NU goalie Jim Bowman's 21. The between-Beanpots game with Dartmouth gave little encouragement to fans who appreciated team defense; BC won 9-7 over the second-echelon Indians.

Team defense was hardly evident in the first period of the championship game. BU had 18 shots on rookie goalie Skidmore. They came up empty. Skidmore totaled 44 saves for the game, and according to the *Globe*'s John Ahern, "at least a dozen were out of this world." Two of the latter were early-on robberies of Mike Eruzione—he of 1980 Olympic Gold medal lore—and three-time All-America player Rick Meagher.

Two seconds before the first period ended, a slap shot by defenseman Kevin Bartholomew made it past BU goalie Brian Durocher and into the BU net. The Terriers had owned the ice, BC led on the scoreboard. Nobody expected it to continue.

In the second period, BC scored two shorthanded goals, 34 seconds apart on the same penalty, to go up 3-0. Senior Richie Smith fashioned his on a breakaway, slithering around the backpedaling BU point man Gary Fay and sending him tumbling to the ice. Bob Ferriter had the other shorthanded score and later put the Eagles up 4-2 with 14:12 to play. Then came more penalties. BC killed off 44 seconds of a 5-on-3, but BU closed to within one with 4:40 to play.

In stepped Mullen to atone for two missed first-period breakaways. The kid from the Sky Rink on New York's West Side, scored the clincher with 3:27 to play and added an empty netter with a little over a minute to go. Along with the stalwart junior Ferriter, the two New Yorkers, Mullen from the city and Skidmore from Long Island, had done the most to bring a Beanpot back to Boston College.

Postscripts to this victory: Bartholomew, scorer of the first BC goal, played only one varsity season as an Eagle. Early in the day of the final game, BC coach Len Ceglarski's car was stolen. He lost his papers, briefcase, and any pregame notes and plans he may have written down. And Gary Fay, the Brookline kid who had been faked out by Richie Smith on one of the shorthanded goals, later entered the coaching field, did well as a recruiter, and got an invitation—which he ended up declining—from Jerry York to come to work as assistant coach at Bowling Green.

HOW THE GREAT BEANPOT BLIZZARD OF 1978 LED TO AN NCAA CHAMPIONSHIP GAME

The news of the Great Blizzard dominates memories of the Beanpot in 1978. The "Storm of the Century" in Boston dumped 23.6 inches of snow on top of the 21.4 inches that had fallen just eighteen days before. Another blizzard would hit less than two weeks later. It was a tough winter, all right, and it wrought havoc with winter sports schedules.

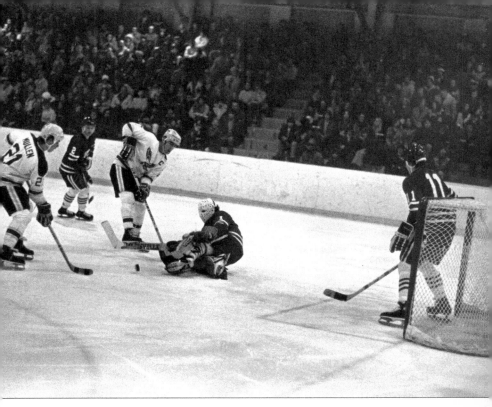

Center Bob Ferriter sets up Joe Mullen with a scoring opportunity in a game at McHugh Forum. (*Photo courtesy of Boston College Sports Media Relations*)

That wave of postponements was a godsend to Boston College. It led directly to a lucky seed in the ECAC playoffs, the playoff championship, and an eventual berth in the NCAA championship game.

The Beanpot title went to Boston University that year. To hockey people in Boston, the Terriers' triumph was as certain as—in the words of former Bruins' general manager Harry Sinden— "death, taxes, and the first minor penalty at Montreal Forum." BU breezed, 12-5 over BC in the first round on February 6. Almost a month later, the Terriers cakewalked over Harvard, 7-1. That same evening, Boston College eked out a win over Northeastern, 3-2 in overtime, in the consolation game. Joe Mullen tipped home a pass from Paul Barrett for the victory.

That consolation win, as it turned out, gave the Eagles just enough of a boost in the league standings to make a playoff spot possible. Had there been no postponement, the Eagles would likely have lost to the Huskies and to New Hampshire in another upcoming game. BC had been struggling in early February. Their first game back was ten days after the Beanpot opener, and BU again romped, this time by 10-5. The Eagles were playing poorly and had lost talented junior goalie Paul Skidmore to a reaggravated groin pull in the first Beanpot game. But Skidmore got back in time for the NU game. He was also in the net the final game of the season, a Sunday afternoon makeup with UNH. He made 49 saves to singlehandedly defeat the Wildcats.

BC thereby avoided a first-round playoff visit to BU and certain elimination. The story of the subsequent march to the NCAA final game, a 5-3 loss to BU, appears in the next chapter. But that story, and the fond memories surrounding it, would never have been told had there not been a Great Blizzard of 1978 on the first night of the Beanpot.

And as for that first night at the old Boston Garden, the storm had been howling for most of day, but 11,686 fans showed up anyway. The Harvard-Northeastern opener lengthened the long evening by going to overtime before Harvard pulled out a win. BU built a lead of 8-4 after two periods of the second game, and the outcome was no longer in doubt. Midway through the second period, the lights began flickering, and there was a 12-minute delay while enough lamps came back on to let the action continue.

Many fans stayed until the bitter end anyway. Garden PR man Nate Greenberg announced over the public address system that the storm was so severe that the Garden would remain open if fans wished to remain and wait it out. Only about 150 people did stick around. Just about every one of those 11,686 who came out that evening has a harrowing tale of the journey home.

The Boston College team bus made it back to the McHugh Forum. Len Ceglarski, who lived in Holliston at the time, borrowed a mattress from sons Peter and Paul, who were living nearby in the lower-campus Mods. Ursula Ceglarski and two other Ceglarski sons walked from the Garden to Len's brother-in-law's house in Watertown. Len slept on the desk in his office for four nights. That Friday, he was finally able to get his car freed and drive home. On his way through Newton Centre, he just happened to see several of his team members pulling a makeshift dining hall tray/sled over the snowbanks. He took a closer look and kept driving. The sled carried cases of beer.

The team was actually a capable bunch. When they got serious about their hockey, they could play with anyone. But they were also a crew of party animals, long before Budweiser's ad agency dreamed up Spuds MacKenzie. After that week of turmoil, the coach decided to give his thirsty players a pass.

THE 1980s:
BREAKTHROUGHS AND BRIEF BALANCE IN THE BEANPOT

The decade of the 1980s was an unusual one in the history of the Beanpot Tournament. It began with Northeastern's first-ever championship that has become the stuff of legend. The Huskies would go on to win four times in those ten years. They and BU co-owned the Beanpot in the 1980s, each taking it four times while Harvard and Boston College had one victory apiece.

The years from 1980 to 1983 comprised the only stretch of time when all teams took turns in winning a Beanpot championship. Each time Boston College played in the final game, winning it once and losing once each to the Huskies, the Crimson, and the Terriers.

The 1980 Boston College team ended up leading the ECAC in the standings. They were good, but hardly fearsome or formidable. They looked sluggish in a 4-3 first-round win over Harvard. The Crimson entered the game 4-10-1, but they bolted out to a 3-0 first-period lead. Third-period goals by Mark Switaj and Gary Sampson pulled the game out for BC.

Northeastern had already knocked off defending champ BU in overtime in the first round. The Huskies were to end up with a terrible record for the season, finishing 7-20. But the good young players were finally arriving for Coach Fernie Flaman. They would win the ECAC and go to the NCAAs two years later. They rose to the occasion in the final against the Eagles in a preview of coming attractions.

Northeastern played like a team possessed. Boston College went out to a 3-1 first-period lead. But after that, the Huskies outshot them 24-14. BC again took the lead when Bobby Hehir scored early in the third period to make it 4-3. Northeastern had a power play late in the period and tied the game on a goal by Paul McDougall with 3:36 to play in regulation.

In the overtime period, Turner dashed up ice as the third man of a 3-on-2 break. Dale Ferdinandi was tripped as he tried to pass off to Larry Parks. The puck went to the uncovered Turner instead. He beat BC goalie Bob O'Connor high to the glove side. O'Connor was starting in place of Doug Ellis after Ellis had been late for a team meeting.

After twenty-nine years of futility, Northeastern had its first Beanpot. They would win three more over the next eight seasons. But in 1981, it was Harvard's turn. Goalie Wade Lau only needed 15 saves in a 2-0 victory over BC in the final, the first time the Eagles endured a shutout.

In 1982, after Chris Delaney's OT goal had let BC escape with a 3-2 OT over Northeastern in the opener, BU stepped in to claim the prize. The Terriers eked out a 3-1 win on the strength of a 40-save show by Cleon Daskalakis. Billy O'Dwyer got BC's only goal and was stopped on several other clear chances by the NU netminder. The loss was the fourth Beanpot final defeat in a row for the Eagles.

The rebuilding 1982–83 Eagles finally broke the losing skein. They dumped Harvard 5-4 in overtime in a first-round game that had been moved from Monday to Tuesday evening because of heavy snow forecasts. Freshman Bob Sweeney assisted on both the tying goal late in the third period and on Ed Rauseo's game-winner in overtime.

Sweeney then was one of seven players who scored in the finale, an 8-2 rout of Northeastern. That BC team finished with an overall winning record of 15-13-2, but it was BC's only Beanpot champion team that did not go on to postseason playoffs.

There's a final, close-to-infamous memory from the 1980s that deserves its own niche in Beanpot lore. As *Attack of the Killer Tomatoes* is to the history of cinema, so is the 1986 team's "Beanpot Trot" music video to Boston College hockey films.

That 1986 team was a good one. They went 26-14-13, finished runner-up to BU in the Hockey East tournament, and got an NCAA tournament berth. Several of them went on to professional hockey.

In January 1986, sports fans around the country had guffawed at the "Super Bowl Shuffle" rap number by the Chicago Bears. After performing their little song and dance, "da Bears" went out and creamed the New

England Patriots 46-10 in the 1986 Super Bowl. So why not emulate the Bears with one about hockey?

In the "Beanpot Trot" video, each of the nine Eagle players, clad in maroon and gold warmup suits and dark glasses, swaggered forward to "sing" eight lines of doggerel. Bob Sweeney, the MVP from three years past, chanted:

"My name is Sweens,
The one with the stats.
I never get excited,
Unless it's over cats.
If you can't find me,
I'll be in the slot,
Movin' my feet,
To the Beanpot Trot."

Scott Harlow, the team captain and third-leading scorer in BC history with 223 points, stepped up with:

"My name is Howie.
You can call me slick.
I don't do much talkin',
But I carry a big stick.
I'm not s'posed to tell you,
My real name is Scott.
I'm just here to dance and do the Beanpot Trot."

And goalie Scott Gordon, one of the best BC has seen—in the net, anyway—belted out:

"My name is Gordon.
They call me Flash.
I'm quick with the glove,
Always on the dash.
And when they score,

It's never a lot.
I'm just here to split
And do the Beanpot Trot."

So it went on for some four minutes, a hilarious parody of the Bears' mocking spoof of the rap "music" genre. The video got leaked to the media and found its way onto the air. Alas, the Eagles did not then go out and sweep to victory like the Monsters of the Midway. Boston University rose to the occasion once again and slapped BC 4-1 in the 1986 final. But fortunately, there's no record of any of those nine Boston College players' trying his luck at show business.

EXORCISING THE DEMONS IN 1994, WILD WEST STYLE

It's heresy to suggest that the Beanpot Tournament has attained the status of a religious ceremony in Boston, that hub of faith and devotion since the Pilgrims landed and started to chase turkeys and hang witches. But sometimes one wonders.

Religious terminology and biblical imagery flowed like the waters of Babylon in February 1994 when Boston College captured two overtime contests against heavily favored opponents to win their first Beanpot in eleven years.

"Ashe Monday" proclaimed the *Globe* headline, signaling not the arrival of Lent but the goal by defenseman Tom Ashe at 8:05 of overtime. The score lifted the 11-13-3 Eagles to a 2-1 victory over Harvard (15-3-1), second-ranked in the country when the puck dropped.

The *Globe*'s Joe Concannon, ever the traditionalist, wrote of "[d]emons of the past exorcised in a victory that may mark the dawn of a new era. . . . Coach Steve Cedorchuk has his first jewel to cherish."

The 1994 Beanpot is a cherished memory for Steve, but he coached just nine more games for the Eagles and ended the season with a 15-16-5 record. It was the only Beanpot victory by a BC team that finished below .500 for the year.

The Most Valuable Player of the tournament was sophomore goaltender Greg Taylor, who'd come to BC all the way from Sherwood Park, Alberta. He was a busy man in the crease for the four seasons he played at the

Heights, and he was never better than in Beanpot '94. He had 26 saves in the final to 23 for Harvard's Steve Israel.

In the opener against favored Northeastern, Taylor stopped 40 scoring chances. The game went to double overtime before senior John Joyce beat NU goalie Mike Veisor with a high 15-footer at 6:52 of the period. Joyce hadn't been feeling great all through the game; he'd just returned from a bout with the flu. He said afterward that a timeout called by the coach shortly before his goal gave him a breather that left him with just enough strength to make the winning play.

The Eagles had gone up 4-2 in the third period on an unassisted goal by freshman Jeff Connolly at 2:16. Connolly played only that one year at BC and then signed a professional contract. His goal wasn't quite enough for an Eagles victory that night. The Huskies tied the game and sent it to overtime with 4:53 remaining in regulation, setting the stage for Joyce's heroics.

The Harvard game looked as though it was going to go the Crimson's way, and right up until the end it seemed to be the best chance for the school to win back-to-back Beanpots. They didn't and still haven't.

Harvard got a power-play goal midway through the second period. Don Chase, who also had a goal in the first game, put home a pass from Rob LaFerriere with 4:32 left to play in the third period. On the game-winning goal, Ashe carried the puck into the zone, waited a split second for help, and just threw a shot on net. Harvard goalie Aaron Israel was moving in the crease, possibly anticipating a pass rather than Ashe's shot, which caught him by surprise.

Boston College's only Beanpot win of the 1990s might have evoked religiously tinted language from the newspaper scribes, but it might have been better described as a Wild West show. All of the heroes were from "out West," at least as far as Bostonians are concerned.

John Joyce, scorer of the winning goal in the double-overtime opening round, came from Wilbraham, Massachusetts. Chase, whose goal beat Harvard in the finale, was from West Springfield. And tournament MVP Taylor's hometown of Sherwood Park is a little less than 200 miles north of where they hold North America's most famous rodeo, the Calgary Stampede.

Taylor was the first Canadian ever recruited to play hockey for BC. He was the goalie for four years, and none of his teams had a winning record.

But as of 2014 he was second all-time in saves for a BC career. In 130 games, Taylor made 3,605 saves.

Career save leader John Muse played in 144 games from 2007 to 2011 and made 3,696 stops. Muse is also the only goalie in Boston College history to be in the goal for two NCAA championship games.

Taylor's status as Boston College's first Canadian recruit gets a small asterisk. Yes, he was the first north-of-the-border native to play varsity hockey at Boston College. But in 1971–72, Snooks Kelley's last season, the Eagles had a promising freshman defenseman from Toronto named Johnny Wintermeyer.

His father, John Sr., was a prominent public figure in Canada. He was leader of the Ontario Liberal Party. After an electoral defeat he became chairman of both the Metro Toronto Catholic High Schools and the Canadian Olympic Association. Young John transferred out of BC after his freshman year. But had he come down one year later, when freshmen began to play on the varsity, Johnny Wintermeyer would have been Boston College's first Canadian.

THE NEW MILLENNIUM AND A NEW ERA:
EIGHT BEANPOT WINS AND COUNTING

Early in his tenure at Boston College, Jerry York was one of the coaches who were invited to speak at a gathering of alumni at Fenway Park. He and football coach Tom O'Brien had both arrived on campus shortly before. They both had multiyear rebuilding programs ahead of them, and the alumni who turned out wanted to let the new coaches know that they'd be supported in all their work and be given plenty of fan support along the way.

In hockey, Boston University was still at or near the top of the sport and utterly dominant in the Beanpot. Terrier coach Jack Parker was frequently the subject of rumor and speculation that he might try his hand at coaching the Bruins. Someone at the gathering asked York if ever hoped that Parker would move on and make a little more room at the top.

York would hear none of it. We want Jack to be there and BU to be at its best, to recruit its best players, and to give us its best shot. And we want to beat them that way, he explained.

It took just as long for Boston College to win its first Beanpot under Jerry as it did for them to win its first NCAA championship of his era: seven years. There's no telling who the opposition in the NCAA Tournament will be in any given year. But the Beanpot is a different story. For the Eagles, Boston University would always be the team to beat. That's why the Boston College team bus, making its way to the Garden for Beanpot competition, drives down Commonwealth Avenue and past Boston University's Agganis Arena first.

York points out that the Eagles could have won a few more along the way before stringing together the five straight Beanpot crowns from 2010 through 2014. He points out that hot BU goaltenders almost always played a role when BU took home the Beanpot. That's true; Terrier netminders won the MVP award five times between 1999 and 2007. Terrier goalie Sean Fields even won it in 2004, a year that BC was champion after a 2-1 overtime win in the final. BC's only goalie to win an MVP award since Greg Taylor did it in 1994 was John Muse in 2010.

Sudden-death overtime was also a familiar refrain when Eagles and Terriers met in Beanpot competition. Between 1992 and 2014, six of the fourteen BU-BC Beanpot games went into overtime, with the Eagles winning four times.

Jerry is the one who dubbed the Beanpot the beginning of "trophy season." When asked about how he prepares his teams for the Beanpot, he said, "It's like the national championship. Once you get a blueprint, you ask, 'How are we going to play on the first Monday in February?'"

This approach echoes remarks by the captain and alternate captain of the 2001 team, York's first to win both the Beanpot and the NCAAs. Defenseman Bobby Allen, summing up the team's approach to the season's preparations after three straight NCAA tournament appearances as well as three straight misses in the Beanpot, said, "We had to break it down into smaller goals. Whatever chance you have to win a trophy, you win a trophy. Whatever we could win that year, we won. That catapulted us into the NCAA Tournament. "

Brian Gionta was even more direct in a postseason media interview, saying, "We just decided that we're going to win everything we played in."

In other words, one thing at a time. And the Beanpot was just one thing. It wasn't everything. In fact, when the team aimed for the Beanpot as the high point of its season in 1997–98, it backfired badly.

Not expecting the run to the NCAAs, which did take place, the Eagles thought that 1998 would be the year that they finally dethroned BU in the Beanpot. They didn't even get to meet the Terriers. Harvard rebounded from a 4-2 deficit in the opener and nipped the Eagles in overtime, 5-4.

Ask anyone associated with that team about the 1998 Beanpot, and you'll most likely hear the word "devastating." But the loss spurred them to channel their anger at themselves into harder work in practice and games, and they didn't lose another one until the national final against Michigan—also at the Garden, as it turned out.

In 2001, the Eagles did not win every trophy available. They finished third in the Great Lakes Tourney in Detroit during Christmas break. But the Beanpot, the team's first in seven years, came back to Conte Forum. Krys Kolanos was the tournament MVP. Two months later, he would score on his classic overtime rush to give BC the NCAA title.

The 2001 Beanpot was truly a team effort. Kolanos scored only one of his team's nine goals. Six other players had goals. Only Kolanos's linemate Chuck Kobasew had two goals in the tourney; six others had one goal as well as the Eagles beat Harvard 4-1 and BU 5-3. "At glorious long last," wrote the *Globe*'s Bob Duffy, "BC has something to show for it."

It was Eagles and Terriers again in the 2003 final. BU goalie Sean Fields was outstanding, turning back 31 shots. He also benefited from a good night of shot-blocking by his mates and the Eagles' inability to click on the power play.

The following year, 2004, Fields became just the second player to win consecutive Beanpot MVP trophies since BC's John Cunniff in 1964 and 1965. But this time the MVP was on the losing team. Fields almost stole the game for the Terriers, making 50 saves in a 2-1 overtime loss.

The Eagles' alternate captain Ty Hennes tied the game at 1-1 with just 3:30 to play in regulation time. Earlier in the period, BC defenseman J.D. Forrest thought he'd scored, but the goal was waved off by referee Scott Hansen, who ruled that the skate of BC's Adam Pineault was in the crease. The winning goal came from Ryan Murphy on a power play.

Tony Voce had drawn a penalty in the overtime period; he put on a burst of speed and was hauled down by a BU defender. Murphy whiffed on a backhander from in front of the cage and the Terriers tried to clear. Ryan Shannon poked the puck back to Murphy, and the junior grinder from Rumson, New Jersey, didn't miss on his second try. BC had outshot the Terriers 52-13 in the game.

The Terriers reasserted themselves as Beanpot dynasts, winning the next three titles. Two of them were over the Eagles, by a score of 3-2 in 2006 and 2-1 in 2007. In the first round of the 2005 tournament, the Terriers also grabbed a one-goal victory when they edged BC 2-1.

The 2008 tournament dawned, and it was time for Boston College to put together a serious Beanpot streak of its own. The Eagles won six of the next seven Beanpots. They defeated Harvard once in the final, in 2008. Three times they vanquished Northeastern, in 2011, 2013, and 2014. Boston University fell victim in 2008 and 2010.

Three times in that championship run, the games went into overtime. On two other occasions when Eagles and Terriers met in the first round, the games went to sudden death before Boston College prevailed.

In 2008's first round, Nathan Gerbe's second goal of the game, at 7:15 of overtime, propelled the Eagles to a 4-3 win. That relegated BU to the consolation game for the first time since 1994. In the final, it was freshman defenseman Nick Petrecki's turn in the two-goal limelight. Nick's second goal of the game and of his college career came at 7:07 of overtime when he put home a Pat Gannon rebound.

After the off-year of 2009, the Eagles were back. Four different players scored to put BC up 4-1. The Terriers rallied late and closed to 4-3 but couldn't get the equalizer past John Muse. With 31 saves, including two sparklers against Nick Bonino in the closing minute, Muse earned the 2010 MVP award.

Muse had 34 saves in the opener the following year. Defenseman Tommy Cross scored on a power-play slap shot at 3:17 of overtime for the winner in a 3-2 Eagle victory. In the final, Jimmy Hayes scored at 7:06 of overtime to give BC a 7-6 win over Northeastern. Chris Kreider scored twice and assisted on Hayes's game winner to earn MVP designation.

In the 2012 final, Boston College had 44 shots on BU goalie Kieran Millan to only 19 against Parker Milner. They needed overtime again, and sophomore Bill Arnold came through with just 6.4 seconds remaining in the extra session when he beat Millan with a shot to the glove side from the right circle.

Goaltender John Muse backstopped the Eagles to two NCAA titles, as a freshman in 2008 and as a junior in 2010. He was also named Most Valuable Player of the 2010 Beanpot. (*Courtesy of Boston College Sports Media Relations*)

Johnny Gaudreau, right, scored a goal in his first National Hockey League game with an assist going to BC teammate Bill Arnold. A few days earlier, Gaudreau became the third Boston College player to receive the coveted Hobey Baker Award. (*Dave Arnold*)

Kevin Roy of Northeastern scored five goals in the 2013 tournament and earned the MVP award. It was only the fifth time that a player from a losing team was selected. BC's Johnny Gaudreau scored twice in the 6-3 triumph. Gaudreau had originally committed to play at Northeastern, but he switched to Boston College when NU coach Greg Cronin moved on.

In the 2014 tournament, BC defeated Northeastern 4-1 in the final. Captain Patrick Brown scored the game winner at 14:30 of the final period. Lying on his back near the slot area, Brown somehow got his stick onto the puck to redirect it past NU goalie Clay Witt. He and Johnny Gaudreau added late goals to widen the margin to 4-1. Senior Kevin Hayes was tournament MVP after scoring a goal against NU and in the 3-1 first-round win over BU.

For "Johnny Hockey" Gaudreau, it would be his final appearance on Garden Ice. The junior from Carney's Point, New Jersey led the nation in scoring, won the Hobey Baker Award, and turned professional, signing with the NHL's Calgary Flames after the Eagles bowed out of the 2014 Frozen Four with a semifinal loss to eventual champion Union College.

For Gaudreau, and for the seniors of the Boston College classes of 2013 and 2014, there had never been a taste of defeat in a Beanpot contest. The Eagles' record since 2010 was ten wins, no losses.

That's one super-sized serving of Boston baked beans!

8

TRANSITIONAL YEARS

"The Times They Are A-Changin'," wrote Bob Dylan of Hibbing, Minnesota. That ballad of social upheaval became the anthem of the 1960s. It was published in 1964, the same year that Dylan's (then known as Robert Zimmerman) neighbor from Hibbing, Jim Green, became the first Minnesota player recruited by Snooks Kelley to play hockey at Boston College. There's an omen lurking somewhere in that odd coincidence.

Ice hockey at Boston College has endured the buffets and turbulence of two world wars and a global economic cataclysm. The teams' responses to those pivotal events are worthy of mention in any history of the sport. But for almost any intercollegiate athletic program, the times of transition that are the most difficult, and which ultimately bring upon the most enduring shifts, are the changes of coaching regime.

The changes to America stemming from the 1960s were profound, and they still echo through the society today. But as the decade was drawing to a close, Boston College hockey was also approaching an inevitable and long-anticipated change of its own: the end of Coach Kelley's 36 years behind the bench.

Of the 68 seasons since varsity hockey resumed following World War II, Boston College has compiled a losing record only 11 times. Of those 11 years, eight occurred within two years of a change in head coaches. A ninth one was Jerry York's third year. The only outliers were the 1957–58 season, a 9-12-2 year, and 1987–88, when massive squad turnover due to both graduation and departures of star players to the Olympics brought on a 13-18-3 season's slate.

There have been three coaching changes for Boston College hockey: Snooks Kelley to Len Ceglarski; Ceglarski to Steve Cedorchuk; and Cedorchuk to Jerry York. The announcement and subsequent departure of Mike Milbury, a roughly two-month period between Cedorchuk and York, added delay and confusion at the time but cannot be considered in the same light as the others.

Additionally, Cedorchuk's tenure only lasted two seasons and came after his 17 years of serving as Ceglarski's assistant and chief recruiter. Therefore, one may consider the six losing seasons from 1991–92 through 1996–97 to be a single era of transition. It took from Ceglarski's final year as head coach through York's third season to reestablish continuity in the recruiting and to reset the team's culture. This should be no surprise. Uncertainty about a college program's future can bring doubts to the minds of potential recruits. If a recruiting pattern is broken and the pipeline dries up, it requires several seasons to restore consistency, reestablish a culture, and return to winning ways.

College hockey was evolving rapidly in the 1990s as well. Many highly competitive programs, such as UMass-Lowell and Vermont, were emerging or upgrading. Adding them to the mix with longer-standing, high-quality rivals such as Boston University, Maine, New Hampshire, and Harvard gave star young players more options and made recruiting all the more difficult.

The game of hockey in America would keep evolving too. More kids were playing youth and junior hockey, skating more hours, getting better coaching than in the past. College-quality players would emerge from unlikely places like Florida, California, and Texas. Better feeder systems would develop and close the experience gap that had given Canadian youth a big advantage in previous decades.

Still, three changes of coaching regime are not the only events that changed the course of Boston College hockey history. As we have seen, the Great War delayed the launch of intercollegiate hockey at Boston College, and the Great Depression curtailed it for four seasons.

WAR BREAKS OUT—BUT FIRST, A NATIONAL CHAMPIONSHIP

Charlie Sullivan '42 graduated from Malden Catholic High, which didn't have a hockey team. But he grew up in Melrose, which had ponds aplenty, and was good enough to suit up and play the game at Boston College.

As Charlie, a third-line center, puts it, "If most of us tried to play today, we'd look like fourth graders. But Ray Chaisson, Fishy Dumont, and Bob Mee could play with any of these guys today. Mee was a defenseman from Melrose and he could skate like Milt Schmidt of the Bruins. He played a whole game against McGill [a 9-3 loss in January 1939]."

In the summer of 1941, Sullivan got a draft board notice informing him that he could be called for army service at any time. The lad spent the summer at Mount Hood golf course, didn't bother to get a summer job, and didn't have his $250 or so he'd need for tuition. So he did not enroll for senior year.

But one day in September he visited the school and encountered Father Lawrence, the dean, near Saint Mary's Hall. Hearing that Sullivan had no money, the priest asked, "You played hockey, didn't you? Go see Father Powers and tell him I want him to give you a hockey scholarship."

That's how Charlie Sullivan got back onto the team. They practiced once or twice a week, usually at 5 or 6 a.m., at Boston Arena. The two-hour practices were almost always games against Northeastern, BU, or the 99 Club, a Boston version of New York's St. Nicholas Club. Saint Nick's, made up of former Ivy Leaguers and Olympic players, was a power in those days.

Sometimes the BC practices would be intrasquad games, with the freshmen plus Chaisson's first line against lines two and three. "We'd play for two bits. Then we'd go buy breakfast at the White Tower on the way back to school," said Sullivan. Most of the players also had part-time jobs at local supermarkets, and they earned extra money by donating pints of their blood to the Red Cross.

The numbers gradually dwindled that year as players shipped out to military service. Sullivan's last game was the season's seventh, a 7-2 loss to Dartmouth at the Garden. But the Eagles finished the year with a flourish. After the 9-2 regular season, they entered the National AAU Tournament and knocked off defending champion Saint Nick's.

For the AAU Tourney, Coach Kelley brought up a trio of freshmen from the squad coached at the time by Bob Mee: Eddie Burns, John Cunniff, and Tom Dolan. In the first game, Jim Edgeworth, John Murphy, and Nick Flynn all scored in a 3-2 victory over High Standard Hockey Club.

The semifinal game against Massena, New York, Hockey Club ended in a 7-7 regulation-time tie after BC blew a three-goal lead. Massena scored early in the ten-minute overtime to take the lead, but Wally Boudreau tied the count on a rink-length rush. Then Harry Crovo, a defenseman from Woburn, scored the winner when he flipped a high, looping backhand shot over everyone in the zone and behind the stunned goalie.

The championship final against Saint Nick's was a seesaw battle that stood 4-4 after two periods. Halfway through the third period, with both tired squads slowing down, Boudreau set up Flynn for the winning goal. Edgeworth added an insurance tally with 18 seconds to play.

Coach Kelley told *Heights* reporter Tom Meagher that the season was "the most glorious year that hockey has ever enjoyed at the Heights, with the local and national titles, backed by enthusiastic student support." Immediately after the final game, Arena manager Paul Brown presented BC captain Ralph Powers with the George V. Brown Memorial Trophy, signifying the National Championship of American Amateur hockey.

HOCKEY'S REVIVAL FOR GOOD IN 1945–46

The Eagles played an abbreviated nine-game schedule in 1942–43 and then closed the sport down for the duration of the war. John Buckley of Malden was responsible for the initial revival of BC hockey. Buckley had played for Snooks from 1938 to 1940 before going into the service. Though Father Joseph Glavin, S.J., is listed as coach in the record books, it was Buckley who issued the "callout" for candidates in late 1945.

Many returned veterans showed up at the Boston Skating Club on Soldiers' Field Road. Buckley was player, coach, and manager. They paid their own money for ice rentals and played against many of the local high schools. They wore castoff BC football jerseys, some of which had "55-12" stitched on the sleeve, a reminder of the score of the devastating 1942 football loss to Holy Cross. They split home-and-home games with Holy Cross and lost 11-0 at Dartmouth. It was a long car ride to Hanover for the outgunned Eagles that day. Dartmouth had a naval ROTC program that had attracted many star athletes, including US Olympians Joe Riley and Cliff Harrison. Eagle goalie John Spinney had 62 saves. The goalie's postgame assessment: "The Eagle laid an egg tonight."

Still, that club team was the bedrock on which Kelley would build his first championship sextet. When Snooks returned from his Navy service,

Buckley worked with him on the transition and became an assistant coach and manager.

THE DEAN OF THEM ALL AND HIS LOYAL SUPPORTERS: THE PIKE'S PEAK CLUB

Coach Kelley went on to direct Eagle fortunes until 1971–72. For 23 of his 36 years behind the dasher, Snooks enjoyed the enthusiastic support of one of college hockey's oldest continually operating booster organizations, the aptly named Pike's Peak Club. Their emergence on the scene also ranks as one of the pivotal transitions in Boston College hockey history.

In the spring of 1949, BC hockey fan Pete Charlton hosted a gathering for the national champs at his 4040 Club in Roslindale. The evening's entertainment consisted of Giles Threadgold's performing a series of Snooks Kelley impressions, to the delight of all including the coach himself.

A couple of months after that memorable evening, three of the players decided to make things official. Bernie Burke, Jimmy Fitzgerald, and John Gallagher met again and established an organization that would promote and support BC hockey as well as recognize the team members' accomplishments.

Those first championship tournaments out in Colorado Springs had taken place fifteen miles east of the majestic pink granite mountain known as Pike's Peak. Katharine Lee Bates had stood on its summit in 1893, and the view inspired her to write "America the Beautiful." Undoubtedly inspired by their own views of that summit from below, as well as by memories of their achievements as America's first Eastern college team to win a national hockey crown, the trio named their organization the Pike's Peak Club. As teammate John Byrne also wrote some years later, "Pike's Peak translated into the Heights that Boston College hockey had ascended."

The original membership requirements were exclusive: membership on the BC hockey team; participation in an NCAA Tournament; and a visit to the Broadmoor Resort in Colorado Springs.

Those narrow criteria couldn't last, and didn't. Only three varsity squads were originally eligible. The Eagles returned to Colorado Springs just twice more before the tournament moved to campus sites beginning in 1959. Over the years all players became eligible to join, followed by season ticket holders and relatives of current players.

The Pike's Peak Club's first annual postseason dinner in honor of the team took place in the spring of 1951 at the 4040 Club. In 1958, with the opening of McHugh Forum, the Pike's Peak Club became the first sanctioned, on-campus club with a room of its own under the stands at the Forum. John "Jay" Mahoney '58 emerged as a hardworking leader and tireless advocate for Pike's Peak during that period. A former hockey team manager, Jay was inducted into the BC Hall of Fame in recognition of his efforts.

Pike's Peak Club dues were set at $25 in 1952. They rose to $50 in 1988 and again to $150 in 1992 to comply with athletic director Chet Gladchuk's requirement that the club be an unsubsidized, income-producing organization. As of press time, annual dues were $250.

The Club now holds an annual season-opening Mass and brunch, "Skate with the Eagles" day for kids, alumni hockey game, and summer golf tournament in addition to its awards banquet. The Pike's Peak Golf Tournament now raises at least $25,000 annually, with proceeds going to hockey program improvements that have included video equipment, computers, and renovations to the locker room and adjoining spaces.

Finally, Pike's Peak pledged $150,000 in 2003 to endow a men's ice hockey scholarship. That commitment represented the largest single gift by a sports-related organization in BC history.

THE CLOSE OF THE KELLEY ERA AND PASSING OF THE TORCH

When the 1969–70 season ended in a 3-8 tailspin and early exit from the ECAC playoffs, a 10-5 quarterfinal defeat by visiting Harvard, that still wasn't enough to make for a losing record. The Eagles finished 16-10 on the year. But with a large and talented—though mostly underperforming at the end—senior class graduating, rocky times lay ahead.

Kelley teams had only suffered one losing season to date in his long tenure. They had never missed the ECAC Division I playoffs by falling out of the top eight. But recruiting had not maintained its pace after 1965, when the Class of 1970 arrived on campus. Both streaks—winning seasons and ECAC playoff qualification—came to an abrupt end.

The 1970–71 Eagles finished 11-15 and suffered several lopsided defeats. Ten of the losses were by margins of more than three goals.

When it was all over, radio color man Bill Bedard opined in a *Heights* article that at least Boston College hockey ended the season with a win, a 5-2 triumph at Army.

Snooks entered the 1971–72 season with 487 career wins. His seniors, particularly Vin Shanley, Scott Godfrey, and Jack Cronin, knew in their hearts that the Eagles would be a second-tier club once again. But they also remembered the senioritis and ignominious finish of their sophomore year.

The Class of 1972 determined that they wouldn't follow suit. Instead, they made it their mission in life to get the Snooker his 500th career win. It would be difficult enough with the returning talent and was made even tougher when Tom Mellor took the year off to play in the Olympics.

The team opened with a three-game tournament in Duluth. The first game was on Thanksgiving, the same day as the college football "game of the century" between Nebraska (35) and Oklahoma (31). The team members decided that they wanted to start the year off right for their coach. They smuggled a cake onto the plane for the flight to Minnesota. The message in the frosting on the cake read, "Giving Thanks for Our Great Coach." Kelley was close to tears at the team meal on Wednesday evening.

The year started auspiciously too, with John Monahan's two goals sparking a 4-3 win over Minnesota-Duluth. *Hey, this might not be too hard*, they thought. Thirteen more wins to go.

It was hard. Exceedingly so. A 2-7 slump whose last game was a 4-2 home loss to Dartmouth between Beanpot games put the Eagles at 9-13. They had to win at least four more times in the last eight games, which included the brutal North Country swing to Clarkson and St. Lawrence, and yet another game with BU, which had beaten the Eagles seven straight times.

They pulled it off, and the Snooker's memorable 500th win over the Terriers has its own chapter in this book. But it took a bit of luck, and the fallout from a preseason political squabble in Eastern hockey, to make it happen.

That fallout was an extra game at Dartmouth, added in September. The ECAC had split down the middle over the "Colgate Proposal," which was to allow freshmen to play varsity hockey. BU coach Jack Kelley announced that he would not, initially, use freshmen but would reserve the right to do so.

That stand prompted Dartmouth athletic director Seaver Peters to cancel his team's game with BU. The first man Seaver turned to for a fill-in game was BC athletic director Bill Flynn. Bill agreed to a February 21 game in Hanover. Sports information director Eddie Miller scrambled to stop the presses that were set to print the season hockey guide so that the extra game could be added.

The schedule looked borderline insane: at Clarkson on Friday, at St. Lawrence on Saturday, fly home on Sunday, bus to Dartmouth on Monday, then home to play BU on Wednesday and Army on Friday.

But the hockey gods smiled this time. At Clarkson, Reardon snapped a 4-4 tie when he tangled with defenseman Bobby Clarke in front of the net, purloined the puck, and stuffed it by goalie Carl Piehl. Ed Kenty added an empty-netter.

After falling to Saint Lawrence and busing back to the hotel through foot-deep snow, the Eagles flew home the next day on the airsickness special. The chartered Air New England DC-3 circled Logan several times, pitching and yawing through the buffeting winds before touching down.

Stomachs had barely quieted before the exhausted team boarded the bus the next day. Fortunately, the heavy snow of the weekend had prevented Pennsylvania from making it to Hanover for their Saturday night game. That contest was delayed until Sunday, which meant that Dartmouth would be playing on two consecutive nights.

This time the hero was center Ed Hayes. He picked up a clearing pass that banked off the neutral zone boards and soloed in on the goalie for the winner in a 6-5 triumph. The Eagles had sewn up a date with destiny, setting the stage for BU. Snooks Kelley's going-away party would be a happy one. As Heights writer Mike Lupica wrote after the 500th win against the Terriers, "The old man had his windmill."

THE HONEYMOON YEAR AND TRANSITIONAL ERA OF THE CEGLARSKI REGIME

The Snooker's sendoff was happy and the Ceglarski years started off well. The Eagles returned to the ECAC playoffs at the Garden and to the NCAAs

Clarkson assistant coach Jerry York, athletics director John Hantz and head coach Len Ceglarski present a plaque to BC head coach John "Snooks" Kelley. (*Photo courtesy of Boston College Sports Media Relations*)

for the first time since 1968. They beat Cornell 3-1, really for the first time ever after 14 straight losses, except for the 24-1 "game" at the Rye, New York, Playland Ice Casino in 1939. The first game with BU was a 7-5 win that gave the Eagles, however briefly, a 51-50-4 lead in the all-time series.

Len had yet to rebuild the recruiting base, but he had a handful of good players to lead the honeymoon year. Future Hall of Famers Ed Kenty and Tom Mellor were seniors, and Reardon was a diligent captain. There were several promising rookies too—Richie Smith, Mark Albrecht, and Mike Powers comprised a dynamic freshman line. The issue of freshman eligibility, such a bone of contention the previous season, had quickly faded from view.

But the roster depth simply wasn't there. Four of the seven sophomores on Kelley's last team didn't play as juniors. At the freshman level, pickings were even slimmer. Of that year's newcomers, only Mark Riley and Richie Hart would play on the varsity for three years.

Things got slowly better after the two down years that followed Len's honeymoon season. In 1975–76, the first Beanpot win in eleven years, the first-ever win over Cornell in Ithaca, an eighth-place finish, and a pulsating 6-5 playoff loss at BU all pointed to better times ahead. Then came a fifth-place finish and another road playoff loss to the Terriers, this time 8-7 in overtime. The ECAC championship year of 1977–78, detailed in chapter 9, came next.

In the background, the team's roster was adapting to meet the new realities of college hockey competition. After the disappointing 1974–75 season, Bill Flynn called Steve Cedorchuk, then head coach at Saint Anselm's College, to see if he'd like to return to the Heights as assistant coach. The Eagles needed more players, and they needed to develop additional recruiting sources.

It was the second such call from Boston College that Cedorchuk had received. The first one had come back in 1965 when Steve, a rugged Townie defenseman, was playing for Boston Technical High of the old City League. He was ready to accept a scholarship offer from Jack Kelley at BU when his friend and former high school rival Jerry York of BC High phoned and asked him to hold off. Snooks Kelley had prevailed upon Jerry, a sophomore at BC at the time, to make the final pitch. Steve waited and got the scholarship offer from Snooks a few days later.

With competition for local talent as fierce as ever, and with archrival Boston University riding high after its two national titles in the early 1970s, Minnesota was the logical place to scout for hockey talent. The more experienced players from north of the border were still not an option at that point, and American junior hockey was still at least a decade away from being a reliable college feeder system.

Cedorchuk was also a Boston schoolteacher. For his first eight years of coaching at BC, he would be at afternoon practice on weekdays and be off to Minnesota on most weekends. Into Minneapolis, south to Rochester, up to Duluth, across to the Iron Range. By the 1979–80 season, there were six Minnesota players on the Boston College roster. "We got the leading scorer of the Iron Range Conference two years in a row," he said proudly.

But even though the new recruiting pipeline from Minnesota was producing talent, Cedorchuk maintained, the pivotal recruit in reestablishing Boston College credibility was Billy O'Dwyer of South Boston and Don Bosco High School.

"Billy was the first player we got in going head-to-head with BU. It took us two years. But when he came, that started us on the road back. A great recruit like him doesn't have an impact for just his four years at the school. It's also felt in the year before he gets here, when other players notice he's coming. Then it's here for two or three years after he leaves, when people who came here because of him are playing," Cedorchuk explained.

O'Dwyer was a freshman in 1978–79, which ended with a (barely) winning record of 16-14. Bothered by a number of factors that included off-ice issues, the Eagles finished out of the ECAC playoffs. They even had home-ice losses to Division II opponents Lowell and Bowdoin.

Nonetheless, the first major transitional era was finally complete. Eleven of the next twelve seasons were winning ones. The losing one, 1987–88, was the 13-18-3 Olympic year that could also be considered a transitional one. Conte Forum was still under construction. It was the second of a two-year homeless stretch, of practices at foreign rinks at odd hours, and of zany stories like the time cocaptain John Devereaux missed the departure of the team van and pedaled a bicycle to practice while dressed in his hockey gear.

"After Billy O'Dwyer came, if we were going after eight kids in a year we'd usually go five for eight. We had some fantastic classes, and we were getting kids with high aspirations," Cedorchuk said, citing the likes of Brian Leetch, Craig Janney, Doug and Greg Brown, Ken Hodge, Tim Sweeney, Marty McInnis, Steve Heinze, David Emma, Scott Gordon, and others.

A CONFUSING POSTSEASON ENDS AN ERA, FINALLY LAUNCHES A THIRD

The five-out-of-eight average for recruiting didn't hold up as the transition away from Len Ceglarski's tenure behind the bench approached. Boston College had established a nice tradition of success at the college level and had sent fifteen players from the 1980s to professional hockey. But that mattered little to aspiring college players of the late 1980s.

The best prospects then, as they are now, were better trained, better coached, and carried more experience than incoming players of any previous generation. They had many options, and they wanted to know who'd be teaching and coaching them for the next four years when they evaluated potential colleges. For a protracted period of time, no one was certain what would happen at the Heights, and recruiting suffered.

The timeline, as reassembled from newspaper stories that followed the unfolding drama, shows that Ceglarski informed athletic director Chet Gladchuk of his intention to retire after one more season sometime in the spring of 1991. That fall, Gladchuk announced that there would be a national search for the best candidate available. Eventually, Cedor did get hired, officially accepting the job on February 25, 1992, at a press conference held in the Shea Room of Conte Forum.

Head Coach Steve Cedorchuk behind the Boston College bench. (*Photo courtesy of Boston College Sports Media Relations*)

The delay had disrupted recruiting flow and affected at least two years of incoming classes. The first year that Cedorchuck coached, 1992–93, saw the Eagles fall to seventh in Hockey East and post an overall record of 9-24-5. The following year was considerably better at 15-16-5, with a sixth-place league finish and featuring a Beanpot championship, the first since 1983.

That improvement wasn't enough for Gladchuk. On March 14, two days after the team bowed out of the Hockey East quarterfinal playoffs, Cedorchuk's resignation was announced. Many newspaper stories put quotation marks around "resignation" to signal their obvious skepticism that the move had been anything but a firing. Years later, Steve said, "I did my best, but it wasn't meant to be. I never wanted to coach anywhere but BC. And I was succeeded by John Wooden."

On March 30, with considerable fanfare, Boston College announced that Mike Milbury would be the school's next hockey coach. It was a dramatic, big-name hire by Gladchuk. A previous hire from pro ranks, Tom Coughlin, had already restored the fortunes of the Eagles' football program. Chet had high hopes for another former NFL coach, Dan Henning, whom he had hired at BC when Coughlin moved on to the Jacksonville Jaguars. So, why not another coach with professional experience?

Milbury had grown up in Walpole and played hockey at Colgate. His mother, Marian, had even been a neighbor of Len Ceglarski back in East Walpole. A fearless, in-your-face defenseman and an erudite, quotable guy off the ice, he'd been with the Boston Bruins' organization for 20 years as player, coach, and assistant general manager. As coach, he led the Bruins to the Stanley Cup finals in 1990 and was named Executive of the Year by the *Sporting News*.

The *Globe*'s Michael Madden wrote that negotiations with Milbury had been going on prior to Cedorchuk's resignation. Gladchuk maintained that the two had not spoken until March 14. Whatever—it was going to be happy days at the Heights once again.

It didn't last. On June 2, Milbury was gone. Through his lawyer, he cited "philosophical differences." He'd never signed a contract, as it turned out. Had he stayed, it would have been quite unlike his former post at the Bruins, where he'd had a good deal of authority and autonomy.

But money also had to be a consideration. Press speculation, which had not been contradicted by any of the parties, had him making something in the area of $150,000 for five years at Boston College. At that time, there were four much more lucrative head coaching jobs open in the NHL: the Islanders, Nordiques, Flyers, and Whalers. Mike coached the Islanders for four seasons, beginning in 1995–96.

So Boston College was without a coach again, and preseason workouts would start in a little over two months. The hockey alumni were not happy. Vin Shanley, president of the Pike's Peak Club, was one who gave Gladchuk a generous piece of his mind, letting his Irish temper run high as he did so. Vin had been Snooks Kelley's last captain. He'd also been coached by Jerry York, a graduate assistant during Vin's time as a player. Shanley was one of many longtime longtime supporters of the program who'd been there through good times and bad. He was also one of the most vocal of those supporters.

To Gladchuk's credit, he listened to Shanley's pointed critique, went home, and phoned Vinnie a few days later to request help in picking the next coach. Shanley agreed. A raft of familiar names and well-qualified candidates of different vintages surfaced. The process quickly narrowed down to a few candidates—it had to, time was short—and York was one of those interviewed by Shanley and others.

"What we needed was a strong, stable hand. That was Jerry. He was forty-six years old at the time. He had the experience. He was a winner. We needed him," recalled Vinnie.

This time, it was easy. Jerry York became Boston College's hockey coach on June 15, 1994. He would succeed at the helm the man he'd helped Snooks Kelley recruit as a player some twenty-nine years before. After a brief detour, the head hockey coaching job was back in the BC family. The new era was set to begin at last.

MAKING THE TRANSITION WORK

Jerry had twice been through the choppy waters of a head coaching change. His first thought was about his players.

"All programs are cyclical to a point," he said. "We had gone through three coaches in a very short duration, with Lenny, Steve, and Mike. We just needed some stability. About a third of that team could have played on any of my teams in the last twenty years. We had some terrific guys, but we just didn't have the depth and the quality on the roster from one through twenty.

"I really wish I could have had some of them seven or eight years later," he continued, citing players like Don Chase, David Hymovitz, and Ryan Haggerty. "But they were very important because they helped stabilize our program, and we slowly started rebuilding."

Rebuilding meant recruiting. And success in recruiting meant reestablishing credibility in the program itself. Boston College had to become, once again, a place where players could enroll with the confidence that they'd both make the most of their individual talents and be part of a winning team.

BC's Marty Reasoner and BU's Chris Drury meet after still another hard-fought game between the Commonwealth Avenue rivals. (*Photo courtesy of Boston College Sports Media Relations*)

As Billy O'Dwyer had made believers of a wave of recruits some seventeen years previously, Marty Reasoner signaled to the hockey world that Boston College was on the way back. A native of Honeyoe Falls in upstate New York, he had starred for Deerfield Academy and had gained international experience with the United States junior national team. He had offers from many schools in all regions of the country. But he'd visited the Boston College campus when his prep school team was in town for a tournament, and he'd wondered why such an impressive place had not been doing better in hockey.

Reasoner changed plans and decided to go to college a year earlier than he had projected. A few months after York took over at BC, he and assistant coach Scott Paluch met with Reasoner at a New York Thruway rest stop near Albany. Marty was headed for the World Junior Team tryouts, and he agreed to meet the BC coaches halfway.

"Coach explained how BC was changed and moving forward, and how they would work on developing the new young guys. He said I'd be able to play in every situation. BC was losing eleven or so seniors that year. Deerfield had been in a similar situation, and I went in and got to play a lot right away. My first year, I played on a line with Dave Hymovitz and Don Chase. They were both really good players, but the guys in that class had been through a lot with three different coaches in four years. They were just trying to find an identity.

"And there were times when it was tough. You want to play with guys who are going pro and having success. And BU was the cornerstone of that in those days. But hockey is a tight world. Word filters down, and people start to come. So in the back of our minds, it was a longer-range plan. We knew that in the first year we'd take some lumps, but by the back end, we'd have success," said Reasoner.

Other recruits in Reasoner's class were Andy McLaughlin, Andy Powers, Chris Masters, and Nick Pierandri. The following year, Mike Mottau, Blake Bellefeuille, Jeff Farkas, and Kevin Caulfield came aboard. Then came the class of 2001, who were seniors on the first Boston College NCAA champion team in fifty-two years.

Jerry York had needed four academic years and three full recruiting seasons to assemble the roster he needed and set a steady, predictable course for the Eagle program. But the competition for top-notch talent was

Coach Jerry York. (*Photo courtesy of Boston College Sports Media Relations*)

fiercer than ever, and even the prospective players who should have taken very little persuasion were never a certainty to choose BC.

Bobby Allen was one of them. He should have been what the admissions office calls a "legacy." He'd grown up attending Boston College games—his peers were either "BC Kids" or "BU kids," and he was the former. His cousin Bobby Ferriter had been a go-to guy for Len Ceglarski's teams of the mid-1970s. One would think that it would take only a form letter to enroll Bobby Allen. It took a lot more than that.

"I wish it was that easy for me. I got offers from a majority of the DI programs. I had narrowed it down to Michigan, Harvard, BU, and BC. BU was one of the top teams in the country. Michigan was in that same class," said Allen.

"I had played against Marty Reasoner. He was light years ahead of everybody else. When Coach York was able to convince Marty to go to school at BC, the next year it was Mottau, Bellefuille, Farkas, and other guys I'd played against. Then it was Gio [Brian Gionta], [Mike] Lephart, [Scott] Clemmensen, [Marty] Hughes, and me. It took a guy of Marty Reasoner's caliber to start it."

"Mike Cavanaugh was the guy who kept after me, always sending me handwritten notes, letting me know that they were going to change the program and bring it back to prominence. In the end, I trusted the coaches. I wanted to be a part of something that brought the program back. But it was much more of a leap of faith for Marty Reasoner than it was for me."

The transition to the Jerry York era was complete, beginning in the fall of 1997. But just as Moses never got to enter the Promised Land, Reasoner never got to hoist the NCAA Championship trophy. He was tricaptain of the 1997–98 team that lost the final in overtime to Michigan, and then he turned professional.

"In a lot of ways, we took the lumps when it wasn't expected," Reasoner said. "We pushed through the barriers and got to the finals. It took a couple of years, but we got there. We didn't win one, but the guys in our class take pride in the fact that we pushed the door open for the others."

9

BOSTON COLLEGE AND THE NCAA TOURNAMENT
The First Half Century

HOCKEY IN A BARN BUILT FOR HORSES—IN THE SHADOW OF PIKE'S PEAK

In March 1947, representatives from nineteen colleges around the country convened at the Lincoln Hotel in New York. They'd been invited by University of Michigan coach Vic Heyliger, whose letter asked, "How does the idea of a national college hockey tournament sound to you?"

It sounded like a great idea, especially after the horrors and tragedies of a world war. It was time for some fun and frolic. Most of the hockey-playing schools of the era were in the eastern part of the country, though, and none of them wanted to sponsor the event. Up stepped Thayer Tutt, a Harvard graduate, hockey buff, and owner of the luxurious Broadmoor Resort and Spa in Colorado Springs. He even got his directors to kick in travel and lodging money.

And so began the NCAA Tournament. It wasn't designated "championship" until 1955. Heyliger, who retired as coach of Air Force Academy after a long career, stated, "With hockey growing the way it was, we wanted to nationalize it. The tournament wasn't run for the money involved. It was more a social event and experience for the players. Everybody enjoyed the parade, the ball, and the beauty contest."

The organizers also had a "branding" ritual in those early years. A souvenir plate of wood was tied around the seat of one's pants and his initials burned into the wood with a branding iron. The little Broadmoor World Arena, a converted riding academy barn with red-carpeted aisles and walls festooned with wildlife paintings and mounted moose heads, was a cozy place.

The NCAA Tournament stayed at the original Broadmoor from 1948 to 1958. Two teams from the East and two from the West took part each year. Boston College was there for the first three tourneys and qualified five times during that first decade.

The Eagles had resumed hockey as a varsity sport in 1946–47 when Coach Kelley returned from service in the Navy. Most of the players had seen wartime military service too. They brought four years of college eligibility to the roster and went 15-3-1.

The 1947–48 team, the first one eligible for the new national tournament, wound up with a record of 14-5. One of the two spots in the hoedown in Colorado would go to the champion of the Quadrangular League—the hockey-playing Ivies. The other Eastern team would represent the loose confederation dubbed the New England League.

The Eagles finished second to Boston University and topped Northeastern 5-4 in the New England League's first round on a long goal by Jimmy Fitzgerald at 5:25 of overtime. Then BC won the Donald P. Sands Memorial Trophy and a trip west by edging favored BU 5-4. Giles Threadgold put the winning goal past netminder Ike Bevins at 9:10 of the third period.

Off to the Rockies the Eagles flew, on a chartered DC-6 airplane along with the Quadrangular League champion Dartmouth Indians. The flight's first stop was Detroit, where they picked up the Michigan team. All three traveling squads arrived in Colorado Springs on the same aircraft.

On March 19, 1948, the Eagles faced 18-2-1 Michigan in the semifinal game. It was a tight contest. The Boston College team, as was Kelley's trademark, was comprised entirely of players from the Greater Boston area. Michigan's team was 100 percent Canadian—with hometowns such as Moose Jaw, Winnipeg, and Toronto dotting the Wolverine roster. Only head coach Heyliger, a thirty-two-year-old native of Concord, Massachusetts, who had been a Michigan hockey star ten years earlier, could claim American citizenship.

The Michigan strategy was to rough up the Eastern players, but chippy defensemen Connie "Badboy" Hill and Dick Startak picked the wrong Eagle as their target. Every time that big Butch Songin touched the puck he was held, chopped, or poked in the ribs by one of the Michigan blueliners. In the second period, Songin received a brutal crosscheck from Hill—this one opening a cut over his eye. He skated to the bench for quick repairs.

Kelley shooed away BC trainer Larry Sullivan, who had moved in to treat the gash. The coach hoped that the show of blood would draw a five-minute major penalty instead of a two-minute minor. His pleas went for naught, as the officials meted out a two-minute sentence to Hill. However, when the officials detected another Michigan cross-check, this one in overtime, it drew an immediate five-minute assessment.

The Eagles built a 3-1 lead by midway through the second period on goals by Threadgold, Bob Mason, and Joe McCusker. The Wolverines rebounded, however, and led 4-3 by the 8:54 mark of the third period. The bespectacled Hill scored three goals—all of them from shots just inside the blue line.

Late in the game and trailing 4-3, Kelley pulled goalie Bernie Burke for an extra attacker, a "daring piece of strategy," according to the 1949 NCAA Hockey Guide. Broadmoor public address announcer T. O. Johnson called the move to the attention of the 2,700 fans. The stratagem worked. The Eagles tied the game with just 50 seconds remaining in regulation play. Jimmy Fitzgerald collected a pass from Warren Lewis and slid it under UM goalie Jack MacDonald.

The game went to a ten-minute overtime period. Michigan's Wally Gacek scored just 18 seconds into extra session. Snooks again pulled Burke from the cage, but Gacek scored on the empty net with 30 seconds left for the final 6-4 margin.

At the end of the game, still smarting from the six fresh stitches closing his head wound and from the rough treatment he had received from his opponents during the entire game, Songin followed the Michigan team right into their makeshift locker room. He announced in no uncertain terms that if anyone in the maize and blue sweaters wanted to take another shot at him they were welcome to try it right now.

The Michigan players sat dumbfounded at the towering player's bold challenge. Nobody moved. Finally, Heylinger rushed up to his unwanted visitor—who by this time was backed up by Threadgold and defenseman Walter DeLorey of Watertown—and pleaded, "Butch, use your head. Get out of here." Seconds later, a pair of Colorado Springs police officers arrived to escort the impromptu BC "committee" back to their own quarters.

"Snooks almost had a coronary when he heard about it," laughed Threadgold.

Nevertheless, the close loss and overall fine performance of his team during the season prompted Kelley to remark, in one of his most-quoted Snooksisms, "This augurs well for the future of Boston College hockey."

THAT FIRST (NCAA) CHAMPIONSHIP SEASON

The Snooker had been right about an auspicious augury. The following year, 1948–49, was Boston College hockey's best ever. The team went 21-1. They practiced at 11:00 on two nights per week as well as at noon on Sundays. Players would also hang around the Skating Club looking for pickup games at all hours, and they skated on local ponds too. Anything to play the game of hockey.

Kelley was not a rigorous tactician or taskmaster. He let his players free-wheel and saved much of his energy for inspirational speeches. Every meeting with Boston University was "The Battle of Commonwealth Avenue" in Coach Kelley's repertoire. And it was always "Coach," to the players, never "Snooks."

The only blemish on the 1948–49 team's final slate was a 4-2 loss at Dartmouth, then at the height of its glory years under Eddie Jeremiah. "The Harps from the Heights," as the Colorado papers would come to call them, were stubborn and unyielding on defense and better than average offensively.

Goaltender Burke, who'd been with a beach demolition squad in the war, played every game but one in three varsity seasons. The defense pairings usually had Songin with John Gallagher and DeLorey with McCusker. The first line featured Lewis, Fitzgerald, and Jack McIntyre. A

John Gallagher and Edward "Butch" Songin were two key players in BC's 1949 NCAA championship. (*Photo courtesy of Boston College Sports Media Relations*)

trio of sophomores, Len Ceglarski, Jack Mulhern, and Fran Harrington, made up the second unit.

The team breezed through the regular season, breaking a sweat just a few times. In the loss at Dartmouth, Lewis twice sent Fitzgerald in on breakaways. Goalie Dick Desmond stoned him both times. The team wasn't helped by the accommodations at rickety Davis Rink; the cement floor at the players' bench, with no rubber matting, dulled BC players' skate blades and made between-period sharpening a must.

The team's players thought that Yale, coached by Murray Murdoch, was the next toughest foe. BC took the game 3-1 in New Haven, with much of the credit going to diminutive forward John Byrne. The Eli had seized command and had the Eagles on the run in the third period. Byrne took a blow to the head from a defenseman. He made sure that the referee saw the

BC goaltender Bernie Burke shares the 1949 NCAA Championship trophy with Coach John "Snooks" Kelley. (*Photo courtesy of Boston College Sports Media Relations*)

blood trickling from his skull, and the resulting five-minute major penalty squelched the Yale comeback.

In a sold-out Boston Arena on January 2, the Eagles beat eventual NCAA foe Colorado College 6-5 in overtime. Byrne tied the game up in the third period and later blew a chance to end it when his pass to a wide-open Fitzgerald went astray. Mulhern got the game winner in the overtime. Both Songin and McCusker played the entire game, according to a letter written in 1996 by Warren Lewis.

The Eagles again won the New England Tourney and headed west. They took only fourteen players along. Byrne and McCusker were hurt. Spare goalie Norm Dailey stayed behind too; junior forward Threadgold would have been thrust into duty if necessary. The Eagles and Indians (Dartmouth would not change its name until the seventies) flew out on the same chartered airplane.

Giles Threadgold, Bernie Burke, and Len Ceglarski join coach John "Snooks" Kelley in preparing to depart for the 1948 NCAA Tournament in Colorado Springs. (*Photo courtesy of Boston College Sports Media Relations*)

Also on that flight was a young Northeastern graduate and radio broad-caster named Fred Cusick. With two Eastern teams playing in the tournament, there would be at least three game broadcasts and enough listeners back home to warrant college hockey's first "national hookup" radio coverage. Cusick's expenses were paid by Boston hockey man and promoter Walter Brown, who found some promotional funds in his profitable Ice Capades business.

The sophomore line took the spotlight in the Eagles' semifinal game with Colorado. Mulhern potted a hat trick, and the stage was set for a rematch with Dartmouth. So confident of a win was Songin that he and Lewis filled their hotel room's bathtub with beer and ice before leaving for the arena. The players had to dress in the hotel too, because the Broadmoor did not have showers in its locker rooms.

Unlike the wide-open semifinal against CC, the championship game was a tight-checking affair. Kelley used only three defensemen; according to an interview with Fitzgerald, Butch played the entire game. The score was tied at 3-3 in the third period when Lewis apparently scored a goal to put the Eagles ahead. The referee disallowed the score, saying he did not see the puck go into the net.

But a couple of minutes later, Lewis and Fitzgerald broke into the zone. Lewis fed Jimmy on the right wing. Fitzgerald's return pass never made it to Lewis; the puck glanced off a Dartmouth defender's skate and past Desmond for the winning goal.

With time winding down, Dartmouth's Joe Riley split the exhausted defense pair of Songin and Gallagher. He soloed in on Burke and shot. Bernie went to the ice and made a skate save. The rebound went right back to Riley, who then tried to roof the puck. Up flashed Burke's leg to bat the disc away and seal the Eagle victory.

After accepting the championship trophy and returning with his team to the locker room, Kelley knelt down and led his players in the Lord's Prayer.

Players from both teams made it to Lewis and Songin's room to share in the postgame celebration. Athletic director John Curley bought Stetson hats for every team member. Back at the Heights he had to explain his extravagance to gimlet-eyed administrators. The Colorado Springs airport was snowed in the next day, so the BC and Dartmouth teams took a steam train to Cheyenne, Wyoming, and flew home from there.

BOSTON COLLEGE HOCKEY TEAM
U.S. COLLEGE CHAMPIONS N.C.A.A. 1949

TRAINER LARRY SULLIVAN, WARREN LEWIS, WALTER DELOREY, JOHN GALLAGHER, BUTCH BONGIN, FRANK SHELLENBACH, JACK McINTYRE, LENNY CEGLASKI, MGR JOHN CONNELLY
FRAN HARRINGTON, JACKIE MULHERN, GILES THREADGOLD, CAPT. BERNIE BURKE, JIMMY FITZGERALD, JACK MAHLER, BILLY WALSH

BC's 1949 team celebrates the NCAA championship. (*Photo courtesy of Boston College Sports Media Relations*)

They arrived a day late, but a crowd of about a thousand was on hand at the airport to cheer both BC and Dartmouth players. There was no on-campus celebration, but Boston mayor James Michael Curley hosted the team for dinner at the Somerset Hotel. Charming and garrulous, Hizzoner first told the players that they were a fine "football" team.

Massachusetts governor Paul Dever also had the Eagles in for a fete at the City Club. This one featured all the stars of the political establishment, and Harvard coach Cooney Weiland was the guest speaker. Perhaps Jack Mulhern's father, treasurer of the state's Democratic Party, had a little something to do with the affair.

CAMEO APPEARANCES AT WILD WEST SHOWS: THE FIFTIES INTO THE SEVENTIES

College hockey's national tournament remained a showcase for the teams from west of the Mississippi throughout the fifties and sixties and well into the seventies. Selection of participants, two from the East

BC's first National Championship Trophy—1949. (*Photo courtesy of Boston College Sports Media Relations*)

and two from the West, was often left up to committees as leagues in both regions formed, grew, merged, and diverged.

Western teams dominated. They comprised older, more physically mature, and much more experienced players than those on the Eastern squads. There were occasional upsets that included Boston College's 4-3 semifinal win over North Dakota in 1965. National rankings didn't exist and intersectional games were few and far between. What happened in the individual leagues up through the playoffs was the priority. The postseason was an extra treat, rather like a football bowl game in some far-off garden spot, a reward for a league season well done.

The East gained ground, but slowly. Between 1967 and 1972, Cornell and BU each won a pair of national titles. Their successes showed that the western teams were not invincible. But it took until well into the 1980s until a rough parity finally took hold in the tournament.

Between 1950 and 1978, Boston College represented the East in the four-team NCAA Tournament field nine times.

Only once, in 1965, did they defeat a Western College Hockey Association team in the semifinal round and make it to the final. In 1978 the Eagles also won a semifinal game and played in the title tilt. But their 1978 semifinal win was against Bowling Green of the improving Central Collegiate Hockey Association.

Boston College played in the NCAA tournament at the old Broadmoor three more times. Each of those trips to the Rockies resulted in a double-digit trouncing in the semifinal game.

BC's 1967 captain Jerry York joins head coach John "Snooks" Kelley and senior manager Paul Chabot on the Eagles' bench. (*Photo courtesy of Boston College Sports Media Relations*)

In 1950, Colorado College avenged is first round loss of a year earlier by thrashing BC 10-3. In 1954, it got worse when Minnesota rolled 14-1. That Minnesota team proceeded to lose the final, 5-4 in overtime, to the first Eastern champion, the 11-man RPI squad coached by Ned Harkness. In 1956, it was Michigan Tech cruising by a score of 10-4 over BC.

Politics and bickering kept the two best Eastern teams out of the 1952 NCAA Tournament. BC was 17-4 and BU was 15-3-1. But the New England League was crumbling; no league playoffs were held because several qualifying teams had withdrawn from them the previous year. The NCAA wanted BU and BC to play off for the right to go west. Both teams refused, so the NCAA picked 16-7 Yale and 15-2 St. Lawrence instead. The Eagles had beaten both of them during the season.

The 1956 year was another in which the East did not send its best team. Clarkson had gone 23-0 and had beaten BC twice. But the NCAA declared seven senior Clarkson players ineligible. They had played on the varsity, as freshmen, in 1952–53 when the ECAC waived its freshman-eligibility rule due to the Korean War. The NCAA didn't recognize the waiver. Len Ceglarski's predecessor at Clarkson, Bill Harrison, elected to stay home rather than try to compete with half a squad.

The NCAA Tournament moved to Minneapolis in 1958 to be part of the one hundredth anniversary celebration of Minnesota statehood. Apparently miffed at the move, Broadmoor management did not welcome the tournament back the following year. The NCAA finals would thereafter be played at campus sites and, later, in large city arenas.

The era of Denver and Murray Armstrong also began in 1958. Between then and 1969, the Pioneers would win five national championships. Murray was the apotheosis of the Western-style college hockey coach. He had played in the National Hockey League before and just after World War II. The Detroit Red Wings cut him from the roster to make room for a young player, also from Saskatchewan, named Gordon Howe.

Armstrong turned to coaching with the Regina Pats, and after five years there he came to Denver and brought most of his older, professionally trained players along with him. Some of the Western schools could give Denver a tussle during those years, but Eastern teams almost always emerged from NCAA games as unrecognizable roadkill.

Murray's recruiting wasn't universally admired out west, however. Michigan, Michigan Tech, Michigan State, and Minnesota all dropped out of the Western Intercollegiate Hockey League (WIHL) to protest his ways, and the league broke up. After the WCHA formed in 1960, Minnesota wouldn't schedule Denver for another twelve years.

When Boston College hosted the NCAA finals at its new McHugh Forum in 1963, ECAC champion Harvard joined in the boycotting. They wouldn't come across the river to play because of Denver's "professionalism." BC, the ECAC runner-up, participated along with Clarkson. In hindsight, it's too bad that the Harvards felt they had to act in such a principled fashion. Their presence at McHugh would have made for superb theater.

Harvard's star player was Crimson immortal Gene Kinasewich, also a Western Canada boy who had the taint of "professional" because he'd gotten paid to play during his younger days. His archrival on Boston College was Jack Leetch, an Eagle Hall of Famer along with son Brian. Jack versus Gene was always an eagerly anticipated, and often lustily physical, matchup.

The 1963 ECAC final had been a wild 4-3 overtime affair with Kinasewich getting the winner against BC goalie Tom Apprille on a breakaway. Harvard wouldn't have won the NCAA, in all likelihood, and probably would have faced Boston College in the consolation tilt. Still, it would have been another memorable clash in a national championship setting, and two of the finest players of their era, Leetch and Kinasewich, might have had one final go at each other.

As for Murray Armstrong, he coached until 1977, but his last NCAA tournament appearance was in 1973. His last win at that level was a 10-4 semifinal rout of Boston College at the Boston Garden. Five years earlier, his Denver team had eliminated the Eagles 4-1 in Snooks Kelley's final coaching appearance in the NCAAs. The close score was deceptive; BC totaled only ten shots on goal.

Not every one of Boston College's NCAA defeats at the hands of Westerners was lopsided. In 1959, at Troy, New York, BC dropped the semifinal game 4-3 to Michigan State.

Politics had kept mighty Denver out of that tournament. With so many teams refusing to schedule them, the Pioneers only had played ten college games. The NCAA Rules Committee, conveniently chaired by Michigan State's Amo Bessone, issued "guidelines" calling for a minimum of 12 games. Bessone's team just happened to make it to the NCAA tournament for the first time. He drew Boston College, and just got by the team captained by Joe Jangro and featuring newcomers Jim Logue in goal, Tom "Red" Martin on defense, and Billy Daley up front.

In their role as hosts of the NCAAs in 1963, the Eagles were easy pickings for North Dakota. The Sioux scored three times in the first 15 minutes and cruised. But it was different two years later at Brown's Meehan Auditorium. The semifinals once again matched up BC and the green-clad Sioux. Brown, the host team, was the other Eastern participant.

Brown had obligingly knocked 25-6 BU out of the ECAC playoff semifinals, then rolled over and played dead while BC won its first ECAC playoff championship, 6-2. The inspired play carried over to the following week when the hustling Eagles surprised the Fighting Sioux 4-3.

As often happens in playoff competition, the kids came through. Sophomore Jerry York scored a pair of goals, classmate Dick Fuller had

another, and John Cunniff tallied the fourth. Goalie Pat Murphy robbed
Dennis Hextall, Terry Casey, and Don Ross on unmolested scoring bids.
The Eagles caught a break when referee Andy Gambucci ruled that Dave
Mazur's stick was more than two feet off the ice when he batted the puck
past Murphy.

The last time that the Eagles got past the NCAA semifinal round in the
four-team tournament was in 1978. Once again they were the ECAC playoff
champion, and once again a team from Rhode Island's capital had helped
immensely by upsetting a highly favored Boston University squad in the
playoffs. It was Len Ceglarski's sixth season. Three juniors were all at the top
of their respective games: Joe Mullen up front, Joe Augustine on defense, and
Paul Skidmore in goal. Rob Riley and Paul Barrett were superb as cocaptains.

BC finished fifth in the regular season and avoided an eighth seed only
by edging New Hampshire 4-2 in a Sunday afternoon game two days before
the playoffs began. That was the year of the great Beanpot blizzard, and the
storm had caused a slew of postponements. Not all games got rescheduled.
RPI coach Jimmy Salfi maintained that he'd tried to find a makeup date for his
game with BU, but, gosh darn it, the trustees of RPI had told him that it would
require the student-athletes to miss too much class time. With the certain loss
to the Terriers avoided, RPI wound up fourth and got to host Boston College.

After absorbing lopsided defeats of 12-5 and 10-5 to BU and 13-3 to
Cornell, the Eagles seemed an unlikely national contender. They rallied
just in time, winning in overtime up at RPI on freshman Paul Hammer's
goal, to make it to the Garden. Boston University was there too, with its
26-1 record and facing seventh-seeded Providence.

The Friars turned the Garden ice into Fantasy Island for an evening
when they knocked off the Terriers 5-1. BC, meanwhile, got two goals and
an assist from Mullen in a 6-4 win over Brown. The following evening,
Mullen again had two goals. Late in the game the Eagles yielded one goal
on a five-minute power play after Charlie Antetomaso had bloodied Friar
John Sullivan's nose in a retaliatory blow. Charlie had just returned to the
lineup after sitting out a dozen games with an injury.

BC's ECAC playoff triumph was the first time that a team from the lower
four quarterfinal seeds advanced to the league championship. Back they
went to Providence for the NCAAs. This time it was to the Civic Center.

BU was there as the East's second seed after defeating the Friars 5-3 in a committee-mandated NCAA quarterfinal. On Good Friday night, the inspired Eagles sprinted out to a 5-0 lead before Bowling Green found its legs and mounted pressure on goalie Skidmore. Iowan Walt Kyle had a pair of scores, Rhode Islander Bill Army tallied one for his hometown fans, and Skidmore came up big whenever the Falcons showed signs of life.

BC could not maintain the magic for the championship game against the reprieved Terriers. BU scored first, but the Eagles bounced back to take the lead. Joe Mullen, much to the delight of a gang of his buddies who'd come up from New York's Hell's Kitchen, tipped home an Augustine slap shot. Then Bobby Hehir beat Jim Craig with a 15-footer.

Another upset seemed possible, but it was not to be. BU got the lead back, 3-2, by the end of the first period. They slowly widened the margin to 5-2 before Steve Barger gave BC some hope with the game's final goal early in the third period. The final 5-3 score was an eminently respectable one for the 24-10 Eagles to put up against the 30-2 Terriers.

That 1978 NCAA Tournament closed out an era in Boston College's history of postseason play. The next time they would be invited to the NCAA dance was six years later. The tournament field would expand to eight teams, then twelve, then sixteen. A Western champion was no longer inevitable. In the thirty-three years between 1981 and 2014, 21 champions would be from the West and 13 from the East. In the last six of those years, an Eastern team would take the top prize five times.

SEVEN TIMES FOILED AS THE NCAA TOURNAMENT BECOMES A TRULY NATIONAL EVENT

In a preview show before the 2014 Frozen Four Tournament, commentators on ESPN bubbled with excitement as they quoted a now-familiar phrase. "We'll be seeing college hockey royalty in this tournament. Minnesota, North Dakota, and Boston College."

As it turned out, it was the lone parvenu in the field, Union College, who won the 2014 NCAA hockey championship. But that did not invalidate the larger point about the Eagles, Golden Gophers, and—up until 2012 when the nickname was dropped—Fighting Sioux. In the 17 seasons between 1998 and 2014, Boston College had made 15 appearances in the NCAA

Tournament. The Eagles won 34 games, made it to 11 Frozen Fours, and took home four championships.

Of the other regal programs, only North Dakota had made more tourney appearances with 16. Maine also had 15, and Minnesota qualified ten times. The only other college hockey team to win more than one NCAA crown in that 17-year stretch was Minnesota, with two. Boston College belongs. But it was a long trek, marked by more than one team's share of plain rotten luck, before they arrived.

After the Eagles lost 3-2 in overtime to Michigan at the Boston Garden in 1998, in a contest that Michigan coach Red Berenson called one of the greatest college hockey games of all time, *Boston Globe* columnist Bob Ryan wrote, "The official sound track of the championship game was 'Hail To the Victors'—this time. The day when the last sound heard at an NCAA hockey title game is 'For Boston' is coming, and it is coming very soon."

That was a bold prediction for a guy of his vintage. Ryan graduated Boston College in 1968. It had been nineteen years before that the Eagles won their first NCAA championship. It would be thirty-three more years before it happened again. Bob Ryan's generation, and the ones that preceded and followed it, had endured a half century of utter frustration.

True, Boston College had fielded several legitimate title contenders along the way. The tournament expanded to eight teams in 1981. It would eventually grow to 16 participants. Between 1984 and 1991, the Eagles made the national tournament seven times. But only twice did they get as far as the semifinal round, and never to the title game.

Six times in that era, Boston College won the Hockey East regular season championship. Twice they won the league playoff crown. But when the NCAA Tournament rolled around, it seemed that the gods of hockey—pagan deities, no doubt—were conspiring against the East's first champions from so long ago. Sisyphus, forever pushing his rock almost to the top of that hill in Hades, could have related to the players, fans, and coaches.

In 1985, Providence's Chris Terreri twice sent the Eagles home disappointed with unconscionably brilliant goaltending. He made 65 saves in the first Hockey East Championship game when the Friars upset the Eagles 2-1 in double overtime. Two weeks later in Detroit he stopped 62 BC shots in a 4-3 triple-overtime Friar win.

After the second of those grand thefts, the dejected team members convened in Detroit's Downtown Athletic Club. Dan Shea, a freshman that year, recalls with fondness a gesture of support and sympathy from athletic director Bill Flynn.

"We're all in there, feeling terrible, most of us drinking beers," said Dan. "Bill Flynn comes in, sees us, and buys all of us a round. Whether we were freshmen or seniors. Those little things, the camaraderie, the solidarity. That meant a lot."

In 1986–87, the first of two years of construction of Conte Forum, the Eagles hosted Minnesota for a two-game, total goals series at BU's Walter Brown Arena. The Gophers' John Blue had 42 saves the first night in a 4-2 win. The next night BC got to a 3-1 lead by midway in the third period, only to yield the series winner on a long fluky shot from center ice. Blue had 36 saves in that game.

In 1989, it was off to a best-of-three quarterfinal round at Michigan State after dispatching Jerry York's Bowling Green squad in a two-game first round series. The Eagles beat the top-ranked Spartans 6-3 the first night. Late in the third period of that game, though, BC's best player, Tim Sweeney, sprained his ankle and could not play the rest of the series.

The Spartans evened the count with a 7-2 win, then scored on a lucky goal to win the rubber match in overtime, 5-4. A shot from the slot area glanced off defenseman David Buckley's skate and fluttered over the glove of goaltender David Littman and into the net. Then in 1990 at the Frozen Four semifinal, Wisconsin prevailed 2-1 when they "raised shot blocking to an art form," as then-captain Greg Brown put it.

It was more hot goaltender play in 1991 when Alaska-Anchorage invaded Conte Forum for the NCAA first round and put a surprise end to the Eagles' season with 3-2 and 3-1 upset wins. Paul Krake of the Seawolves had 43 saves the first night and 39 the second. That BC team had tailed off through February, however, and lost in the first playoff round to visiting, eighth-seeded Northeastern.

Perhaps the end of 1990–91, with its three consecutive home-ice defeats, was a harbinger of difficult times. The Eagles had not lost even two games in a row at home since Conte Forum opened.

A large contingent of talented players led by Hobey Baker Award winner and all-time leading scorer David Emma graduated in 1991. Six losing seasons, and six years without an NCAA Tournament bid, ensued: Len Ceglarski's final year as coach, two campaigns under Steve Cedorchuk, and the first three years of Jerry York's tenure.

But better times lay ahead. Coach York's Bowling Green team had won the 1984 championship in Lake Placid, 5-4 in four ten-minute overtimes, over Minnesota-Duluth. They'd gotten to the finals by upsetting Boston University in a two-game, total goals series. The new coach had been all the way to the top. He and his new team would get there again.

10

THE REVIVAL
Coach Jerry York

Like a lot of student-athletes everywhere, eighteen-year-old Tom Mellor showed up at Boston College as a freshman in the fall of 1967 with a single focus: playing hockey. "One day, I had heard that Bobby Orr, who was coming back from knee surgery, was going to be skating down at McHugh Forum," said Mellor. "So I cut my classes and hopped on the ice to skate with him.

"I was starting to struggle with my classwork when freshman practice began in October," Mellor admitted. "Then one day, a graduate assistant who was helping out with the team sat me down and said, 'Tom, I want your class schedule right now, and I want you to come back and see me again tomorrow.'"

Mellor assembled the academic information, passed it over, and wondered what would become of all this. "When I came back the next day, he had color-coded my entire week, hour-by-hour," Mellor recalled. "My classes were in one color, study time in another, then lunch, breaks, library time, and finally, practice. He said, 'Now, I want you to come back to me every week and tell me exactly what you did.'

"My studies began to turn around immediately," said Mellor, a future All-America defenseman, member of the US Olympic medal-winning team, and a professional hockey player who today is the CEO of a highly successful investment firm.

"He recognized that I was not putting the effort in. He could recognize a problem, break it into little pieces, and solve the problem. He was incredibly helpful in getting me to turn things around."

The graduate assistant was Jerry York.

* * *

York grew up in nearby Watertown—one of ten siblings—where his father, Dr. Robert York, was the physician to the Jesuit community in Weston. On winter afternoons Dr. York would often bring young Jerry along as he made his medical rounds, and the youngster would skate on the local pond with the resident Jesuit seminarians.

Jerry later went to Boston College High School. "At the time, you would go to BC High with the feeling that BC or Holy Cross was going to be your destination. With hockey at BC and none at Holy Cross then, I always wanted to go to BC."

York recalls the day that legendary BC coach John "Snooks" Kelley asked him to play for the Eagles. "We were just chatting before a game at the old McHugh Forum, and he said, 'I'd love for you to come to BC.' He never mentioned a scholarship," laughed York.

"I was just thrilled for a chance to walk on. I was just so excited."

York had a sterling playing career under Kelley's tutelage, earning All-America honors before graduating with a degree in business administration. He scored the winning goal in his first Beanpot game. He scored twice in an NCAA tournament win over North Dakota. That was the only game where BC defeated a team from the WCHA in NCAA play before he became the Eagles' coach. His teammates elected him captain in his senior season.

After narrowly missing a spot on the US Olympic Team for the 1968 Winter Games in Grenoble, York returned to BC to pursue a master's degree in education. He secured a graduate assistantship to supervise the University's then-tiny intramural program and also helped out coaching the freshman hockey team.

He was sitting in the hockey office one day when Len Ceglarski, another BC grad who was head coach at Clarkson College, called looking for a freshman coach for his staff in Potsdam. The twenty-five-year-old York jumped at the opportunity. Almost.

"My fiancée was Bobbi O'Brien—a niece of Fr. Charlie Donovan, who was the dean of the School of Education," York recalls. "I had to convince her to go to upstate New York. It was no small task getting her from West Roxbury to Potsdam."

The saga ended well: "We got married that summer, and I started up at Clarkson."

Two years later, Ceglarski was named Kelley's successor at BC and York was promoted to top man at Clarkson. At twenty-seven, he was the youngest head coach in Division I college hockey. He won 125 games over the next seven years. From there, York and his family headed to Bowling Green State University in Ohio, which, he proclaimed, was "a good career move and a bigger program."

Over the next 15 seasons, he led the Falcons to 342 victories and the 1984 national championship. He also picked up a valuable piece of coaching advice from Bob Johnson, a legendary collegiate coach at the University of Wisconsin and future NHL head man.

"Bob's son, Peter, was a graduate assistant for us," York recalls. "When we won the title there, Bob called me and said, 'The best thing about winning your first national championship is that it will help you win others. You know how hard you have to work, the types of players you will need, and how to handle the big stage.'"

Johnson went on to explain what he meant. As it turned out, he was telling York that he'd need to do essentially what Jerry had done for Tom Mellor many years before: break everything down into its component parts, and then make those parts fit and work together.

Whether it was a semester's academic schedule for an individual player, or a full year of preparation and execution for a Division I college hockey program, the principle was the same. Jerry already operated that way. Bob Johnson just let him know how valuable it was to do so.

"In the euphoria of winning the national championship, with all the celebrations and parades, I hadn't really sat down and thought, *How did we get to this point?*" Jerry explained. "It was a terrific insight to our program.

"And Bob was right. Once you've won one, and you analyzed it, keep in mind you're not going to win every year, but it's going to help you win the next one. If you've won one, and come up with a blueprint that you can replicate, you'll win more national championships."

What are the individual items that make up said blueprint? Training camp. Day-to-day management. The types and mix of players on the roster. How the team handles big-game pressures. How they travel. The individual goals and milestones set out during the season. How the team plays in its defensive zone. The impact of the senior leadership. The impact of the incoming freshmen. Among many others.

"The names change, and the years go by. But that's the basic core of how we would develop our teams at Bowling Green and at Boston College. The whole thing about building a team is to have great contributions from a lot of different people—with senior leadership, really good goaltending, a structure during the season where we don't overwork or underwork kids, and get to a peak around March," stated York.

So Boston College hockey's road back to prominence on the national scene did not begin on June 15, 1994, the day Jerry York became head coach. It really commenced a decade earlier, in Lake Placid, New York.

When Gino Cavallini tucked a backhand shot past Rick Kosti at 7:11 of the fourth overtime to give Bowling Green a 5-4 win over Minnesota-Duluth, Jerry had his first national championship. Remembering that friendly advice from Bob Johnson, he carried his blank blueprint form to Conte Forum.

The new coach set about filling in the blueprint. It took three years to return to winning ways and six years to capture the NCAA championship. While it may be oversimplifying the story to say so, the two principal ingredients to the Eagles' rebound were the players that wore the uniforms and the approaches that those players brought to the task at hand.

The record in Jerry's first year was 11-22-1. It ended with a 5-4 home-ice loss to UMass in a play-in game for the final Hockey East playoff berth. The next season started off in a discouraging fashion too, with a 7-12-3 record by mid-January. But the reinforcements had started to arrive, and they got the chance to learn college hockey on the job.

Marty Reasoner was Hockey East's Rookie of the Year and collected 45 points, the same as linemate and captain David Hymovitz. Freshmen Chris Masters, Brendan Buckley, Nick Pierandri, Andy Powers, and Matt

Jerry York coaches his Boston College team. (*Photo courtesy of Boston College Sports Media Relations*)

Mulhern all played regularly. The freshman class was the team's most productive one, with 110 total points.

The numbers that the new men put up were not half as important as the mindset they brought. They wanted to win and thought they were good enough to do it. Though he was their classmate, Andy Powers was really a member of the old regime. Powers admits that he needed—and received—an attitude adjustment from his classmates.

Andy's father John had captained Snooks Kelley's second-to-last team, an 11-15 contingent that had been overmatched and outgunned by just about everybody. Andy had been recruited by Steve Cedorchuk, who told him there would be a scholarship waiting if he could go play a year of junior hockey somewhere after high school. Though he managed to stick on the BC varsity and elevate his own game, Andy Powers was the last of the old-style Boston College recruits.

"Guys in my class, particularly Marty, had competed at such a high levels and played with a lot of confidence. They had played in the US junior program and on the world stage. Before them, we never looked at national rankings or thought that we'd be part of it. That confidence they brought was contagious, and it was kind of foreign to us. I think that Coach York inherited a few guys who were just used to losing," said Powers.

Jerry and his staff worked hard to evaluate and bring in the right mix of players—some with size and strength, some with speed and skill. But all of them had to be willing to subordinate their own egos and goals for the good of team and program—even while developing their individual abilities to the highest possible level. That's easy to conceive, but very difficult to accomplish when you're working with youngsters who've gotten used to applause and accolades.

BC stars Brian Gionta (right) and Hobey Baker Award winner Mike Mottau celebrate an Eagle goal. (*Photo courtesy of Boston College Sports Media Relations*)

The harder one works, the luckier one becomes. At times the coaches got lucky out there on the recruiting trail. The second wave of talent brought Jeff Farkas, Mike Mottau, and Blake Bellefeuille. BC's interest in Farkas brought the coaches exposure and early introduction to his younger linemate on the Niagara Scenics. That linemate, from Rochester, New York, came along the following year. His name: Brian Gionta.

Mottau hadn't even responded to the hockey staff's questionnaires and seemed destined to go to Boston University. A Mottau family friend tipped off assistant coach Mike

Cavanaugh that, in fact, the lad wasn't yet committed to becoming a Terrier. York then scouted Mottau at a local Labor Day weekend tournament and was immediately sold on his eventual second Hobey Baker Award winner.

Another time, Cavanaugh was in New York checking out a goaltender when he noticed a defenseman they'd never seen: Rob Scuderi. Scott Paluch went to a Canadian junior all-star tournament to look for goalies and came back with a notebook on a forward from British Columbia named Chuck Kobasew. Greg Brown made two trips to Waterloo, Iowa, to vet defenseman Patrick Wey. On both occasions, Waterloo's lightly used second-string goaltender suited up and played well: Parker Milner.

Marty Reasoner was the player who did the most to restore the Eagles' stature to those outside the program. But as Coach York sees it, the transformation wasn't complete until Gionta arrived on the scene to work his magic from the inside.

"We were getting good players, but the key to it all was Brian Gionta's coming. He brought the competitive spirit of practices and games to a whole new level. He pushed Marty, and Farkas, and Bellefeuille, and he was just a freshman. He went to four straight Frozen Fours," said Jerry.

Gionta's classmate Bobby Allen agrees, remarking, "Marty was creative, more smooth, slower paced. Gio was a bull in a china shop. If you got in his way he'd run you over. Both in their own ways were exceptional leaders, and we all looked up to Gio, with what he'd do with the size he was and his work ethic." These and a few others were the earliest of the big names, the all-leaguers and All-Americas in the early years of Boston College's resurgence. More would follow: Gerbe, Atkinson, Whitney, Gibbons, Gaudreau, Boyle, Kreider, and others. But high-profile star players are not enough to make for a complete, consistent, and reliable team.

Terry Francona, the man who managed the Red Sox to two World Series titles, came in and spoke to the 2011–12 team that went on to win the NCAA crown. He told the players, "When your role players are your best leaders, that's when you're going to have success."

Tommy Cross, captain of that squad, said, "That's what happened with us. It's easy for star players to buy into what a coach is saying. Guys who aren't playing that much can always question what's going on. That didn't happen. It was the exact opposite."

Cross cited swingman Brooks Dyroff, who'd won the 2011 Hockey Humanitarian Award, and third-string goalie Chris Venti, as inspirational leaders.

"They talk about NHL locker rooms with the one guy everybody rallies around. For us, that year, it was Venti. Before every game, after the national anthem when we huddled around the goalie, Venti was the guy with the microphone. He was the one that was getting us ready. Yes, he probably wanted to be playing more. He battled, and he was competitive. All he cared about was for us to be winning."

If you ask Jerry or any of his lieutenants, past or present, about the kind of people they seek for the Boston College program, discussion invariably comes around to a player's willingness to subordinate his individual desires and become part of something bigger.

"If a kid comes in thinking, *How many minutes am I going to play, what's my role going to be?* it's hard to build a team," Jerry explained. "But you've got to become a part of the team or you won't get any minutes on the ice. It's a lack of egos that we want here.

"A lot of the onus is on the individual player. They can't all be Gerbes. Sometimes it takes a while to sort it out, but smart players do. We've got good players in our programs, good people, and they understand it. They've got to want to win championships. We haven't had many players leave, because they do want to be a part of it, so they retooled their game."

Occasionally the appropriate role calls for a player to change his position. Forwards Brian Boyle and Danny Linell moved back to defense. Defensemen Andy Powers and Marty Hughes played up front. But more frequently, the adaptability comes when a high-scoring player finds his best opportunity as a checker.

Sometimes, that scorer-turned-checker returns to his former role. Chris Collins killed penalties and blocked shots for three full seasons and totaled 59 points. Then in 2005–06 he went back on the attack and amassed 62 points in a single year. It's always possible to do more—whatever's needed.

For some, the need to rethink their game was immediately obvious. Others took longer to make the switch.

Matt Greene came to Boston College in 2004 after a high-scoring career at BC High. He expected that to continue, but it only took one practice session to tell him that things would be very different in college hockey. He adapted and wound up on one of the team's best checking lines of the decade.

"When I got to my first captain's practice, I knew very quickly that the game had changed. I remember one pass somebody gave to Pat Eaves. It was about knee-high and an absolute bullet. He just dropped it down out of midair and went in and scored on Matty Kaltiainen. I realized then that the game had picked up a lot," recalled Matt.

"The way it turned out. . .sure, I did lack some offensive play that I previously had. But with Matt Price and Pat Gannon, we carved out a niche within the team. I had a lot of pride in what we were doing. None of us had much offensive clout, but if we were the home team, and their first line comes on, we're going out without even getting a tap on the shoulder."

Greene was elected assistant captain of the team that won the 2008 NCAA championship. His shutdown linemate Price eventually became captain of the 2010 title team. For Price, embrace of a role change came more slowly.

He didn't play at all for the first 13 games of his rookie season of 2006–07. He'd been upset and frustrated at being left off the travel squad for two games at Wisconsin in October. On the Saturday when his teammates were away, Price skated at Conte Forum and scored plenty of goals on an empty net. The BC football team happened to be playing at home that day, the weather was rainy, and many fans had come inside. They cheered loudly whenever Matt would shoot the puck into the cage. It stung.

"I was an offensive playmaker and power-play guy; never did much defense or penalty kill. Early on, they didn't look at me that way. The top three lines were set and only fourth line roles were available. It took me a while to figure it out. I had to simplify my game and work on a few things in practice.

"I didn't think of leaving, but I was a scholarship guy and not playing. I'm sure the coaches would have liked to take the scholarship back at that point," he recalled.

Even though he'd not gone to Wisconsin, Price was waiting for the team bus when it pulled up at Conte Forum on Sunday. Unpacking the bus was the freshmen's job. That little gesture impressed the coaches and showed how much Matt wanted to be a part of the team.

He finally got into the lineup in the first week of December and stayed there. A month or so later, the checking line of Price, Greene, and Pat Gannon made its debut. In the NCAA semifinal game, a 6-4 win over North Dakota, they shut down the trio of T. J. Oshie, Jonathan Toews, and Hobey Baker Award winner Ryan Duncan. The following year, also in the national semifinal, they again blanked Toews and Oshie in a 6-1 BC win.

All-America defenseman Greg Brown controls the action. (*Photo courtesy of Boston College Sports Media Relations*)

As York's lieutenant Greg Brown chuckled, "Wisconsin had Toews and Oshie. We had Greene and Price."

Price remained a defensive specialist for the rest of his BC career. He scored a total of 18 goals in 148 games. But like many others, his contributions could not be measured in goals and assists.

"It wasn't the storybook tale I was expecting," he said. "But guys have to form into the type of player the team needs if they're going to be successful. For me, being a third-line center and playing a role that not everybody wants to play—it was something that I relished."

When Jerry York looks back on the chat he had with Bob Johnson in 1984, he was careful to point out that doing what Bob advised would not bring an NCAA championship every single year. But laying out the blueprint and getting the right people on board would make it easier to get another, and then another, national title as the years went by.

Expectations, then? How about to be a team that must be taken seriously every single year, a team that's always capable of going all the way in any given season. Stay in the competitive mix, and you'll win your share.

That was not the case back in the 1997–98 season. Yes, the rebuilding was underway. A third class of recruits had arrived to compete for slots on the 15-19-4 team from the previous season. But no one was thinking seriously of playing hockey in April, when the Frozen Four would return to Boston for the first time in twenty-four years.

In December 1997, the notices went up on college bulletin boards everywhere. "Spring Break in Cancun! Get your tickets now!"

Several Boston College players anted up. They'd never been to Spring Break, and they wouldn't be playing in the Fleet Center that weekend, would they? But at the last minute, they hedged. Just to be sure, they—Marty Reasoner, Chris Masters, Mike Mottau, Kevin Caulfield, and Andy McLaughlin—booked flights for Sunday, April 5, or Monday, April 6.

Those players came within an overtime goal of either forfeiting their break money or missing a national championship celebration. The Eagles made it all the way to the last game of the college season and lost 3-2 to Michigan in one of the fiercest, most memorable college games ever played.

The 18,276 fans saw BC twice take the lead and Michigan twice tie the score in regulation time. Caulfield in the first period and Mike Lephart in the second put the Eagles up a goal. Each time, Michigan's Mark Kosick countered with goals of his own, the second one with 6:48 to play.

In the overtime, Boston College had three golden chances to win. Senior Jamie O'Leary rang a shot off the crossbar. Jeff Farkas hit a post. Lephart was unable to snag and convert a feed when goalie Marty Turco was out of position. Then with 2:09 to play in the extra session, a shot from freshman John Langfeld sneaked between Scott Clemmensen's skate and the right post.

That team, which nearly went all the way in its first turnaround season, had originally set its sights on a Beanpot win as the highlight of the year. They were cruising along with a 4-2 lead in the third period of round one when Harvard popped home a pair of goals, the tying one with the goalie pulled and 25 seconds left. Then the Crimson won 5-4 in overtime.

"That Beanpot was a devastating loss. For us, we had not been in the mix for national titles, so the Beanpot was our championship. It made us reevaluate as a group. From that point on we just decided it wasn't acceptable to be average anymore," said Reasoner.

The Eagles didn't lose another game until the finale with Michigan. But they did receive one more memorable coach's message—this time from a rival. After BC had defeated Maine 3-2 for the Hockey East championship, Black Bears' mentor Shawn Walsh paid them a locker room visit. He congratulated them on the win and then said, "Don't be satisfied with this. You are good enough to go all the way to the national championship. All you have to do is win three more games."

Walsh had built Maine into a fearsome college hockey power. For the rest of his life, which sadly only had three years remaining, he would oppose the Eagles in high-stakes contests. He was right in his evaluation and was one of the first people on the outside who believed that Boston College was headed for great things. All of the players who heard him that evening came to believe it as well.

It took three more years. The following season, out in Anaheim, Walsh's Maine team edged BC 2-1 in overtime. BC had a 1-0 lead through two periods but couldn't hold on. They had finished third in Hockey East, won the playoffs, and did all the heavy lifting in the NCAA Regionals. They went to Wisconsin and defeated Northern Michigan and a rested, top-ranked North Dakota 2-1 on back-to-back nights before heading directly to California.

In 2000, it was the Fighting Sioux's turn to end BC's season. For the third time in their history, the Eagles sought the NCAA title in Providence and made it to the final round. North Dakota rebounded from an early deficit and controlled play for most of the second and third periods, scoring the winner with 5:38 to play.

Once again, the Eagles first went west to the regional and knocked off the top-ranked team in the country when they beat Wisconsin 4-1. First they got by Michigan State 5-4 on an overtime power-play goal by Farkas. They had tied that game with 50 seconds to play when Lephart tipped home a slap shot by Mottau.

For those who'd return yet again for the 2000–2001 season, losing in the Frozen Four was getting mighty old.

Allen, the defenseman and cocaptain, said, "We had come so close but were still so far away. We knew we had a great group of freshmen and that our senior class was a good one to lead the younger players.

"For us it was just unfinished business. No excuses. We had to find a way to win this thing. We had the national title as our goal, but we had to break it down into smaller goals. Every time you have a chance to win a trophy, then win a trophy. That would catapult us into the NCAA tournament."

The Eagles won the season-opening Great Western Freeze Out, the Beanpot, and the Hockey East regular season and playoff championships. Gionta was the team's leading scorer, but the youngsters were coming along, particularly freshmen Tony Voce, Ben Eaves, and Chuck Kobasew and sophomore Krys Kolanos.

As fate would have it, Boston College would play each of the teams that had eliminated them from the NCAA tournaments over the previous three years. The Eagles defeated Maine, 3-1, in the East Regional in Worcester. Kobasew scored the game winner, his ninth of the year, with 6:15 to play. Rob Scuderi added a power-play goal with just under three minutes remaining.

Maine coach Shawn Walsh was ejected from the game by referee Steve Piotrowski for protesting the penalty call. It was Walsh's last appearance in the game of hockey. Already showing the effects of renal cell carcinoma, a rare form of cancer that had been diagnosed the previous June, he would only live for another six months. Walsh's team's 5-4 overtime win against Minnesota to qualify for the regional final with the Eagles had been the 399th of his career.

Next up was Michigan in the semifinal game at Albany. The freshmen, Kobasew and Eaves, each scored twice in a 4-2 victory. Here it was, another chance to win it all, and the competitive fires throughout the squad were at their hottest. In fact, they almost got a little too hot, and the ones who were nearly singed around the edges were Kobasew and the tourney's eventual game-winning hero, Kolanos.

Krys centered a line with Voce and Kobasew on the wings. He'd had a one-on-one meeting with Mike Cavanaugh the night before the championship game. According to Mike, Kolanos had not been playing up to his capabilities. But there was more to it.

As Kolanos reccalled it, "We were practicing a couple of days before the big game, and I was giving it to Kobasew because I was a little frustrated with how he was playing. He shoots the puck a lot and doesn't pass much, and I was yelling at him because I'm a competitive guy too.

"Cav stepped in, and he and I exchanged some words too. Tensions were running high. So Cav and I had a meeting that night before the game. We put behind whatever had happened because we needed to focus and go forward. I don't think it was a negative thing. It was good that we had a meeting to focus those competitive energies.

"Then, ironically, Kobasew gives me the puck in the neutral zone and gets the assist on the winning goal."

The Eagles looked like they were in command, holding a 2-0 lead late in the game. A penalty for too many men on the ice gave the NoDaks a power play, and they capitalized with a tip-in by Tim Skarperud with 3:42 to play. Then Sioux coach Dean Blais pulled his goalie, and Wes Dorey tied things up with 36 seconds left. The momentum was all North Dakota's when the final horn sounded.

Then came a breather and an inspired locker room pep talk from senior defenseman-turned-forward Marty Hughes. This time, victory would be theirs. The film clip of Kolanos's game winner is one of the most frequently repeated NCAA Frozen Four highlight plays. The sophomore center took

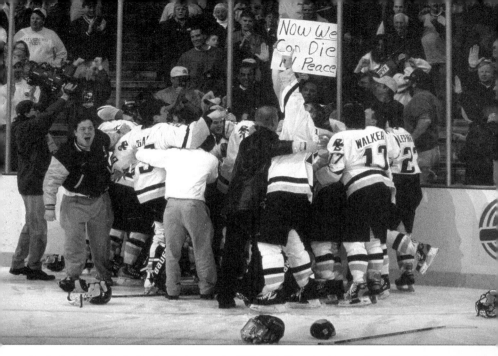

One fan's sign says it all after the Eagles won the 2001 NCAA Championship—ending a 52-year-long title drought. (*Photo courtesy of Boston College Sports Media Relations*)

the feed in center ice, dashed down the left wing, cut to center behind the defense, and stuffed the puck past Sioux goalie Karl Goehring.

The wait was over. Four long years for the seniors. Fifty-two longer years for the BC faithful. It was an end, and it was a beginning. Three more national championships in the next eleven years would have seemed, at the time, a bold and rash prediction. But actually, with a little bit of puck luck, there might well have been at least two more in that span.

In 2006, a youthful Eagle squad blew both Miami and BU away by 5-0 scores in the Worcester Regional and headed west. In the final they took on a loaded, veteran Wisconsin team in Milwaukee. The game ended 2-1 in favor of the Badgers. Defenseman Peter Harrold's last-second slap shot beat the goalie but banged off the post, and the Eagles couldn't quite rally to tie the game.

In 2007, however, Boston College brought a veteran team to the Frozen Four. For the second consecutive year they dispatched North Dakota in the semifinal round. This time the final game opponent was

Michigan State. BC held a 1-0 lead on a Brian Boyle goal until midway through the third period. The Spartans tied it on a power-play goal and took advantage of a BC defensive miscue to break in after a center zone faceoff and score with 18.9 seconds left.

So once again, in the fall of 2007, the Boston College upperclassmen had the dual task of marshaling their troops and beating back any residual pessimism from the preceding two seasons' disappointments. They succeeded brilliantly, because the most unlikely, most unforeseen of all the Eagles' national championship runs came in 2008.

The team's final record was 25-11-8. In the NCAA final, Nathan Gerbe almost singlehandedly vanquished North Dakota 6-2 and Notre Dame 4-1. York stated, "Nathan carried the whole team on his back in that series."

True enough, but that was hardly the entire story. The team started fast, winning seven of its first ten games. For the rest of the regular season, though, the Eagles went a mediocre 10-9-7. They absorbed a 6-1 pasting from Northeastern in the first round of the Beanpot and had to beat the Huskies in the season's final game in order the get the fourth and final home playoff spot. At 17-11-8, BC was not a good bet to go back to the Frozen Four for the third consecutive year.

But Gerbe and captain Mike Brennan had set the stage for the just-in-time turnaround at the team's embarrassing 5-1 loss at New Hampshire late in February. Upset over an errant pass, the fiery Gerbe chewed out the passer and slammed his stick against the dasher. What Brennan recalls as a "heated conversation" with his good friend and former teammate on the US National Under-18 Team began right then and resumed in the locker room between periods.

"It was a conversation with just the two of us even though all the other guys were there. There were no secrets in our locker room. Things weren't going great. For me as captain, there had to be a little turning point. There's a time to be firm and a time to be softer, and that was the time was to have it out a little bit. Fortunately it worked out. Sometimes those situations don't."

Coach York had actually lit that powder keg's fuse a month earlier after a 3-3 tie at Maine. Not pleased at all with his team's performance, he spoke of the Frozen Four.

"I'm going to Denver," he said. "It's up to you if you want to go with me."

"Those specific words I remember. That was an eye-opener. In New Hampshire, I remember coach just sitting there and listening. He didn't say anything. He just let it sit," said Brennan.

"That's the great thing about Coach. He has such a good pulse on the locker room. It reflects on the guys. And when you talk about leadership and captaincy, you learn that it's your job to reinforce the tradition and the history of what BC hockey has become."

And so the Eagles lost four of their last six games, staggered into the playoffs, and never lost another contest. In the Hockey East semifinals at the Garden, they came back from a 4-1 second-period deficit and got by New Hampshire 5-4 in triple overtime. Benn Ferriero's power-play goal 53 seconds into the third session was the winner.

At the NCAA regional final in Worcester, it was another overtime, 4-3 against Miami, that sent the Eagles to Denver. Halfway through the extra session, Miami had been so dominating that York called a timeout. Three minutes later, Joe Whitney put home a Dan Bertram rebound.

There would be no more cardiac-kids games. At the Frozen Four, Gerbe's hat trick and three goals led the way in a 6-1 romp over North Dakota. In the 4-1 final against Notre Dame, Gerbe figured in all the scores, with two goals and two assists. Perhaps he felt he had something additional to prove. He'd been one of three finalists for the Hobey Baker Award and was passed over.

Co-captain Dan Bertram had been assisting Father Tony Penna at the pregame Mass when he inadvertently delivered a sign from heaven that all would go well against the other Catholic institution. Dan was the extraordinary minister serving the Precious Blood to communicants when the glass vessel holding the sacrament suddenly shattered right in his hand.

Father Penna quickly assured the horror-struck Bertram that it was not a bad sign; in fact, it was a good omen because it showed the strength that Bertram would soon be displaying on the ice. Dan finally calmed down but remained nervous. "I didn't sleep a wink when I was supposed to be taking a nap before the game."

Brennan summed it up, "Maybe we weren't the best team in the tournament, but we came together at the right time. By the time we got to the Frozen Four, we knew we had the blueprint."

Blueprint. There's that word again. Learn what works and what doesn't, and plan accordingly. The 2008 Eagles had lost in the national final in both the previous two years. For Brennan and his classmates, the memory of 2007's 3-1 loss to Michigan State was especially bitter.

"The year before that against Wisconsin [a 2-1 loss in the final], they were stacked, we were young, and we played them in Milwaukee. But against Michigan State we went in as the favorite. We thought we were going to do it, and they ripped our hearts out.

"So I never let go of that championship trophy. I had it under my arm all night and in the charter plane the next day."

Following a fifth-place finish in Hockey East and an 18-14-5 overall record for the 2008–09 season, the team captains had an eclectic set of memories on which to build. There had been a bitterly disappointing loss in an NCAA final, a national championship, and a subpar campaign. Where to go next?

Matt Price and his alternate captains, Matt Lombardi and Ben Smith, didn't quite know what to expect when they convened for a preseason brainstorming session. They'd all had the opportunity to witness team leadership in times of crisis, with the Brennan-Gerbe drama in 2008. They'd also have a chance to tap Brennan for his advice just before the Frozen Four.

The record in 2009–10 ended up a much improved 29-10-3, but the season had more than a few rocky moments while the captains sorted things out. They came to learn that personal chemistry means a great deal to team leaders and those they must motivate and prod to do their best.

"We had ten freshmen coming in, and that's a wild card right there. I think maybe we underestimated the talent, because ten guys on the team played in the NHL. But we decided that we'd have to identify early on just who would play what roles. Then they could get better at it throughout the year. I thought we did a pretty good job with that," said Price.

Brian Gibbons and Cam Atkinson rocketed to the top of the scoring heap that season and received good backup from Ben Smith, Joe Whitney, and Jimmy Hayes.

"We as leaders found that we'd gravitate toward certain guys and vice versa. So if there was an issue, we'd know who would be approaching who. Just about all of our offense came through Gibbons and Atkinson, and one time Cav had been all over the two of them, and they were sensitive to how they were being treated.

"I ended up taking them to lunch at CitySide and letting them know that I needed them to be my arms and to carry out what I'm trying to accomplish."

The team finished second in the league and won the playoff championship with a 7-6 overtime victory over Maine. The Bears tied the game up in the last minute, but the Eagles escaped on Lombardi's third goal of the game. There was more escaping at the Worcester regional. The Eagles prevailed but looked sluggish and sloppy in defeating Alaska-Fairbanks 3-1 and Yale 9-7.

Price called his old teammate Brennan for advice. Mike, then playing in the Chicago Black Hawks organization, advised Price and mates to back off a bit.

"He said that we'd got to decompress a little and can't be straight out for two weeks. Take the foot off the gas. Then we had a team meeting at the hotel the night before the first game. As captains, we spread it all out, and there was a leave-no-doubt mentality that we just hadn't yet been playing the way we were capable."

The team's 2010 Frozen Four performance was as close to perfection as any BC team had ever played. Miami, top-ranked and the best defensive team at 1.84 goals per game, fell victim 7-1 to a balanced attack with six different players scoring.

In the final against third-ranked Wisconsin and its potent offense, BC goalie John Muse only had to make 20 stops. Muse became one of the few goalies in NCAA history to be in net for two NCAA championships. Price, the captain, scored the final goal of the final game of his career into an empty net to make the score 5-0.

In the 2011 NCAA Tournament, Colorado College pulled a huge upset in the West Regional's first round by knocking off the favored Eagles, who finished the year at 30-8-1. But in 2012, Boston College was right back at the pinnacle, winning their fourth NCAA title in eleven years and putting up a 33-10-1 record.

The shorthand version of the season's saga tells of the bus ride home from two losses in a weekend at Maine. There was a team meeting, a new resolve, and not another loss for the rest of the year. Nineteen straight wins and the national championship.

Parker Milner capped off an extraordinary year in goal with a pair of shutouts in the East Regional, 2-0 against Air Force and 4-0 over defending NCAA champ Minnesota-Duluth. Then he yielded just two goals at the Frozen Four when BC breezed by Minnesota 6-1 and Ferris State 4-1.

The team captain, Tommy Cross, pointed out that the turnaround-after-Maine narrative is true but is hardly the entire story of the team's success that season. The scoring was potent and balanced with Chris Kreider scoring 23 times, Barry Almeida 22, and Johnny Gaudreau 21. Four others scored goals in double figures, five experienced defensemen played, and Milner had a1.6 goals-against average.

"As leader of the team I just didn't have to worry about big egos. Kreider could have had 60 points, but he was all about playing the right way. Three weeks after we finished he was making headlines in the NHL. I think Brian Dumoulin had more points in his sophomore year, but he was playing the right way. We were all on the same page," said Cross.

"After Maine, looking back on it, we should have been that good. We always talk about practicing at a super high pace. In my sophomore year we had guys like Price and Barry Almeida, when our speed was through the roof. So we started saying this is how we should be doing it, let's not go back to what Brownie [Coach Brown] calls 'coin flip' hockey.

"We got that speed going in my senior year too. We decided we'd practice at a very high pace so that the games seemed slow. Some teams are physical, some have their power play. And sometimes those things don't show up. But your speed is there every night. So for us, it was our depth and our speed."

In the NCAA semifinal, Milner played one of his best periods and held Minnesota at bay with a number of good saves in the first period. BC swung into gear after that and rolled to a 6-1 final, with Paul Carey scoring twice.

The final against Ferris State was a little tougher. Milner earned series MVP honors with a 27-save show. The teams traded goals early, and Carey got the actual game winner at 10:33 of the first period when he deflected home a wrist shot from the point by Dumoulin.

Ferris played stout defense, however, and the score remained 2-1 until late in the third period when Gaudreau scored the highlight-film goal of the year to clinch the victory. "Johnny Hockey" outraced a back-checking wing, toe-dragged the puck around a defenseman, and roofed a backhander.

Cross, obviously a man who values continuity, said later, "When you come to BC, you come to win, to chase hardware and hang banners. You know of the traditions. You know of the guys who've come before you: Marty Reasoner, Brooks Orpik, Brian Gionta. You don't want to let them down."

During the 2012–13 season, York, who by then had been a Division I head coach for 41 years, became the winningest coach in the history of college hockey on December 29, when the Eagles defeated Alabama-Huntsville, 5-2, in the consolation round of the Mariucci Classic Tournament played in Minneapolis. It was his 925th career victory, surpassing the total number of wins of retired Michigan State mentor Ron Mason.

University officials scheduled a "Jerry York Night" gala at Conte Forum on January 18 to celebrate the accomplishment, but BC was forced to cancel the ceremony when York had to undergo eye surgery and was forced to miss several games. York, who never sought or liked the glare of fame's spotlight, was pleased when the recognition ceremony was downsized and postponed to the opening night of the following season.

We leave the final words to Matt Greene and Dan Bertram, alternate captains behind Mike Brennan on the overachieving 2008 national champion team. Both have moved on from playing hockey and are building their careers in the financial services industry.

Bertram fondly tells of the "Dyson Duty," which is one of Jerry York's disciplinary measures for minor infractions. A player who messes something up gets a week of cleaning the dressing room with a top-of-the-line Dyson vacuum cleaner.

"Coach loved the Dyson vacuum, and he was meticulous about a clean dressing room. The next day he'd come in and know if you'd done it or not. As quirky as he was sometimes, he taught me not to cheat on the little things. Whether it was looking professional, with a haircut and no beard, or in practice, making crisp passes and doing every drill at game speed. Now, in the real world, I know that you don't try to cheat the system."

Bertram adds, "I've been on fifty different hockey teams. It's very hard to find a team where you can look around and say, 'These guys do things, and treat people, the right way.' At BC, yes they had to be good hockey players, but just as important, they went out and did the little things in life the right way too."

Greene said, "When we won that championship in '08, it was not because we were the best team. But there was a feeling of family there, that you'd cut your arm off for the guy next to you. Until you're in the room, you don't know what it feels like.

"And when you leave that place, after being a part of Coach York's family, you're so much more groomed for the real world. If you're not five minutes early, then you're five minutes late."